THE COMPI

DIABETIC COOKBOOK

Ultimate Guide of Flavourful Health Management, Nourishing Recipes and Expert Tips, 30 Days Meal Plan Included

BY ALBAN RAY

THE COMPLETE DIABETIC COOKBOOK

Ultimate Guide of Flavourful Health Management, Nourishing Recipes and Expert Tips, 30 Days Meal Plan Included

CONTENTS

CHAPTER I. INTRODUCTION

A. EXPLANATION OF DIABETES AND ITS IMPACT ON DIET

Diabetes is a chronic medical condition when the body cannot properly regulate blood sugar levels. The hormone insulin, produced by the pancreas, plays a crucial role in this regulation. Insulin helps glucose (sugar) from our food enter the body's cells, which are used for energy. In diabetes there are two main types:

- Type 1 Diabetes is an autoimmune disease where the body's immune system mistakenly attacks and destroys the insulin-producing cells in the pancreas. As a result, people with Type 1 diabetes require insulin injections or an insulin pump to manage their blood sugar levels.
- Type 2 Diabetes occurs when the body becomes resistant to the effects of insulin or does not produce enough insulin to meet the body's needs. It is often associated with lifestyle factors like poor diet, lack of physical activity, and obesity. While Type 2 diabetes can sometimes be managed through lifestyle changes, it may also require medication or insulin in more advanced cases.

Impact of Diabetes on Diet: Diabetes significantly impacts diet because the types and amounts of food a person eats directly influence blood sugar levels. Individuals with diabetes need to be mindful of the following aspects of their diet:

- Carbohydrates: Carbohydrates are the main source of glucose in the body. Diabetics need to be cautious about their carbohydrate intake to avoid rapid spikes in blood sugar levels. The focus should be on choosing complex carbohydrates in whole grains, legumes, and non-starchy vegetables rather than refined sugars and processed foods.
- Sugar: Added sugars and high-glycemic foods can cause sudden increases in blood sugar levels. Diabetics should limit their consumption of sugary beverages, candies, desserts, and processed foods.
- Fibre: Fibre-rich foods can help slow glucose absorption and control blood sugar. Including high-fibre foods like fruits, vegetables, whole grains, and legumes is essential for managing diabetes.
- Protein: Protein-rich foods like lean meats, fish, tofu, and legumes can help stabilise blood sugar levels and provide a feeling of fullness.
- Fats: Healthy fats found in avocados, nuts, seeds, and olive oil are important for overall health and help stabilise blood sugar levels. Saturated and trans fats should be limited to protect heart health.
- Portion Control: Monitoring portion sizes is vital to prevent overheating and maintain steady blood sugar levels.
- Regular Eating Schedule: Consistent meal timings can help manage blood sugar levels and avoid extreme fluctuations.
- Hydration: Staying hydrated is important for overall health and can help manage blood sugar levels.

Individuals with diabetes should work closely with a registered dietitian or healthcare professional to create a personalised meal plan that suits their health needs, lifestyle, and blood sugar goals. By making informed food choices and following a balanced diet, individuals with diabetes can effectively manage their condition and improve overall well-being.

B. IMPORTANCE OF MANAGING BLOOD SUGAR LEVELS THROUGH DIET

is crucial for individuals with diabetes and those without the condition. Here are the key reasons why it's essential:

- Diabetes Management: For people with diabetes, consistently managing blood sugar levels is the cornerstone of their treatment. By making mindful food choices, monitoring carbohydrate intake, and avoiding excessive sugars, they can prevent dangerous spikes and dips in blood sugar levels that could lead to complications.
- Preventing Hypoglycemia: Hypoglycemia, or low blood sugar, is a serious condition that can lead to dizziness, confusion, and in severe cases, unconsciousness. By eating regular, balanced meals, individuals can avoid sudden drops in blood sugar levels.
- Preventing Hyperglycemia: Hyperglycemia, or high blood sugar, can occur when the body doesn't have enough insulin or doesn't use it effectively. Uncontrolled hyperglycemia can damage blood vessels and organs over time, leading to diabetic complications like nerve damage, kidney problems, and eye issues.
- Weight Management: A balanced diet can help individuals maintain a healthy weight or achieve weight loss, vital for diabetes prevention and management. Excess body weight can contribute to insulin resistance, making it more challenging for the body to control blood sugar levels.
- Cardiovascular Health: Proper blood sugar management can significantly reduce the risk of cardiovascular diseases, such as heart attacks and strokes. High blood sugar levels can damage blood vessels, increasing the risk of atherosclerosis and other heart-related issues.
- Energy Levels and Well-Being: Stable blood sugar levels contribute to better energy levels, focus, and overall well-being. Avoiding rapid fluctuations in blood sugar can help individuals feel more energised throughout the day.
- Diabetes Prevention: For individuals without diabetes, maintaining healthy blood sugar levels through diet can significantly reduce the risk of developing Type 2 diabetes, especially if they have other risk factors like a family history of diabetes or being overweight.
- Quality of Life: Effective blood sugar management allows individuals with diabetes to lead a better quality of life, as they can minimise the condition's impact on their daily activities and enjoy a more active and fulfilling lifestyle.

By adopting a balanced and nutritious diet, monitoring carbohydrate intake, and making healthier food choices, individuals can control blood sugar, reduce the risk of diabetes-related complications, and improve their overall health and well-being. It's essential to work with healthcare professionals, such as registered dietitians or diabetes educators, to develop personalised meal plans that meet specific health needs and lifestyle goals.

C. GENERAL GUIDELINES FOR CREATING DIABETIC-FRIENDLY RECIPES AND PRODUCT LISTS

Creating diabetic-friendly recipes and product lists involves considering the nutritional content of ingredients and their potential impact on blood sugar levels. Here are some general guidelines to remember:

- Choose Low Glycemic Carbohydrates: Opt for carbohydrates with a low glycemic index (GI) that have a slower impact on blood sugar. Examples include whole grains (quinoa, barley), legumes (lentils, chickpeas), and non-starchy vegetables (leafy greens, broccoli).
- Limit Added Sugars: Avoid using refined sugars and natural sweeteners like stevia, erythritol, or monk fruit extract. Alternatively, use fresh fruits or unsweetened applesauce to add natural sweetness.
- Use Lean Proteins: Incorporate lean protein sources like skinless poultry, fish, tofu, and low-fat dairy products to help stabilise blood sugar levels and promote satiety.
- Prioritise Healthy Fats: Choose sources of healthy fats, such as avocados, nuts, seeds, and olive oil, while limiting saturated and trans fats.
- Increase Fiber Content: Include high-fibre foods like vegetables, fruits, whole grains, and legumes, as fibre can slow down glucose absorption and improve blood sugar control.
- Be Mindful of Portion Sizes: Pay attention to portion control to avoid excessive calorie and carbohydrate intake.
- Emphasise Fresh Ingredients: Use fresh and minimally processed ingredients to maximise nutrient content and avoid hidden sugars and unhealthy additives.
- Flavour with Herbs and Spices: Use herbs and spices to add flavour to dishes instead of relying on excessive salt or sugar.
- Promote Balanced Meals: Ensure recipes balance carbohydrates, proteins, and healthy fats to help regulate blood sugar levels and maintain energy.
- Avoid Processed Foods: Minimise processed and packaged foods, as they often contain added sugars, unhealthy fats, and high sodium levels.
- Read Labels Carefully: When selecting commercial products, read labels to check for added sugars, hidden carbohydrates, and unhealthy fats.
- Include Nutrient-Dense Foods: Choose ingredients that offer a wealth of nutrients and vitamins to support overall health.

Here is a sample diabetic-friendly product list:

- Whole grain flour (e.g., almond flour, coconut flour, whole wheat flour)
- Fresh or frozen vegetables (e.g., broccoli, spinach, cauliflower)
- Fresh fruits (e.g., berries, apples, citrus fruits)
- Lean proteins (e.g., skinless chicken breast, turkey, salmon, tofu)
- Low-fat dairy products (e.g., Greek yoghurt, low-fat milk)
- Nuts and seeds (e.g., almonds, chia seeds, flaxseeds)
- Healthy oils (e.g., olive oil, avocado oil)
- Natural sweeteners (e.g., stevia, erythritol, monk fruit extract)
- Herbs and spices (e.g., basil, oregano, cinnamon)
- High-fibre grains and legumes (e.g., quinoa, lentils, chickpeas)
- Sugar-free condiments and sauces (e.g., sugar-free ketchup, mustard)
- Fresh herbs and spices (e.g., thyme, rosemary, turmeric)

By following these guidelines and using the right ingredients, you can create delicious and diabetic-friendly recipes that contribute to better blood sugar management and overall well-being. Remember to consult with a healthcare professional or a registered dietitian for personalised advice and meal planning based on individual health needs.

D. 30 DAYS MEAL PLAN

DAY 1:

- Breakfast: Scrambled eggs with spinach and cherry tomatoes.
- Lunch: Grilled chicken salad with mixed greens, cucumbers, and a lemon vinaigrette.
- Dinner: Baked salmon with asparagus and quinoa.

DAY 2:

- Breakfast: Greek yoghurt with sliced strawberries and a sprinkle of almonds.
- Lunch: Turkey and vegetable stir-fry with brown rice.
- Dinner: Vegetable curry with tofu served over cauliflower rice.

DAY 3:

- Breakfast: Overnight chia seed pudding with raspberries and a drizzle of honey.
- Lunch: Lentil and vegetable soup with a side of mixed greens.
- Dinner: Baked chicken breast with roasted Brussels sprouts and sweet potato.

DAY 4:

- Breakfast: Avocado and poached egg on whole-grain toast.
- Lunch: Quinoa and chickpea salad with cucumbers, tomatoes, and feta cheese.
- Dinner: Stuffed bell peppers with lean ground turkey and quinoa.

DAY 5:

- Breakfast: Smoothie with spinach, banana, almond milk, and chia seeds.
- Lunch: Greek salad with grilled shrimp and feta cheese.
- Dinner: Baked cod with steamed broccoli and wild rice.

DAY 6:

- Breakfast: Cottage cheese with pineapple chunks and a sprinkle of cinnamon.
- Lunch: Spinach and feta stuffed mushrooms with a side of mixed greens.
- Dinner: Turkey meatballs with zucchini noodles and marinara sauce.

DAY 7:

- Breakfast: Oatmeal with sliced apples, walnuts, and a dash of cinnamon.
- Lunch: Roasted vegetable quinoa bowl with hummus dressing.
- Dinner: Grilled steak with roasted cauliflower and a side salad.

DAY 8:

- Breakfast: Scrambled tofu with bell peppers and onions.
- Lunch: Mexican black bean salad with avocado and lime dressing.
- Dinner: Baked chicken thighs with green beans and mashed cauliflower.

DAY 9:

- Breakfast: Peanut butter and banana smoothie with almond milk.
- Lunch: Spinach and ricotta stuffed bell peppers.
- Dinner: Eggplant Parmesan with a side of mixed greens.

DAY 10:

- Breakfast: Yogurt parfait with mixed berries and granola (sugar-free).
- Lunch: Chicken and vegetable soup with a side of raw carrots.
- Dinner: Baked tilapia with lemon and herbs, served with quinoa.

DAY 11:

- Breakfast: Chia seed and berry smoothie with almond milk.
- Lunch: Greek yoghurt chicken salad with celery and grapes.
- Dinner: Stir-fried tofu with broccoli and snap peas, served over brown rice.

DAY 12:

- Breakfast: Almond flour pancakes with sugar-free maple syrup and fresh berries.
- Lunch: Lentil and vegetable curry with a side of cucumber raita.
- Dinner: Baked cod with lemon and dill, served with steamed asparagus.

DAY 13:

- Breakfast: Scrambled eggs with sautéed mushrooms and spinach.
- Lunch: Quinoa and black bean stuffed bell peppers.
- Dinner: Grilled chicken breast with roasted sweet potatoes and green beans.

DAY 14:

- Breakfast: Overnight oats with almond milk, chia seeds, and sliced peaches.
- Lunch: Tofu and vegetable stir-fry with a side of edamame.
- Dinner: Baked salmon with broccoli and quinoa.

DAY 15:

- Breakfast: Greek yoghurt with raspberries and a sprinkle of crushed walnuts.
- Lunch: Lentil and vegetable soup with a side of mixed greens.
- Dinner: Stuffed bell peppers with ground turkey and quinoa.

DAY 16:

- Breakfast: Avocado and poached egg on whole-grain toast.
- Lunch: Quinoa and chickpea salad with cucumber, tomatoes, and feta cheese.
- Dinner: Baked chicken breast with roasted Brussels sprouts and sweet potato.

DAY 17:

- Breakfast: Smoothie with spinach, banana, almond milk, and chia seeds.
- Lunch: Greek salad with grilled shrimp and feta cheese.
- Dinner: Baked cod with steamed broccoli and wild rice.

DAY 18:

- Breakfast: Cottage cheese with pineapple chunks and a sprinkle of cinnamon.
- Lunch: Spinach and feta stuffed mushrooms with a side of mixed greens.
- Dinner: Turkey meatballs with zucchini noodles and marinara sauce.

DAY 19:

- Breakfast: Oatmeal with sliced apples, walnuts, and a dash of cinnamon.
- Lunch: Roasted vegetable quinoa bowl with hummus dressing.
- Dinner: Grilled steak with roasted cauliflower and a side salad.

DAY 20:

- Breakfast: Scrambled tofu with bell peppers and onions.
- Lunch: Mexican black bean salad with avocado and lime dressing.
- Dinner: Baked chicken thighs with green beans and mashed cauliflower.

DAY 21:

- Breakfast: Peanut butter and banana smoothie with almond milk.
- Lunch: Spinach and ricotta stuffed bell peppers.
- Dinner: Eggplant Parmesan with a side of mixed greens.

DAY 22:

- Breakfast: Yogurt parfait with mixed berries and granola (sugar-free).
- Lunch: Chicken and vegetable soup with a side of raw carrots.
- Dinner: Baked tilapia with lemon and herbs, served with quinoa.

DAY 23:

- Breakfast: Chia seed and berry smoothie with almond milk.
- Lunch: Greek yoghurt chicken salad with celery and grapes.
- Dinner: Stir-fried tofu with broccoli and snap peas, served over brown rice.

DAY 24:

- Breakfast: Almond flour pancakes with sugar-free maple syrup and fresh berries.
- Lunch: Lentil and vegetable curry with a side of cucumber raita.
- Dinner: Baked cod with lemon and dill, served with steamed asparagus.

DAY 25:

- Breakfast: Scrambled eggs with sautéed mushrooms and spinach.
- Lunch: Quinoa and black bean stuffed bell peppers.
- Dinner: Grilled chicken breast with roasted sweet potatoes and green beans.

DAY 26:

- Breakfast: Overnight oats with almond milk, chia seeds, and sliced peaches.
- Lunch: Tofu and vegetable stir-fry with a side of edamame.
- Dinner: Baked salmon with broccoli and quinoa.

DAY 27:

- Breakfast: Greek yoghurt with raspberries and a sprinkle of crushed walnuts.
- Lunch: Lentil and vegetable soup with a side of mixed greens.
- Dinner: Stuffed bell peppers with ground turkey and quinoa.

DAY 28:

- Breakfast: Avocado and poached egg on whole-grain toast.
- Lunch: Quinoa and chickpea salad with cucumber, tomatoes, and feta cheese.
- Dinner: Baked chicken breast with roasted Brussels sprouts and sweet potato.

DAY 29:

- Breakfast: Smoothie with spinach, banana, almond milk, and chia seeds.
- Lunch: Greek salad with grilled shrimp and feta cheese.
- Dinner: Baked cod with steamed broccoli and wild rice.

DAY 30:

- Breakfast: Cottage cheese with pineapple chunks and a sprinkle of cinnamon.
- Lunch: Spinach and feta stuffed mushrooms with mixed greens.
- Dinner: Turkey meatballs with zucchini noodles and marinara sauce.

CHAPTER 2

BREAKFAST RECIPES

1. AVOCADO AND POACHED EGG ON WHOLE GRAIN TOAST

Servings: 2
Prep time: 10 minutes
Cooking time: 5 minutes

Ingredients:

- 2 slices of whole-grain bread
- 1 ripe avocado
- 2 large eggs
- 1 teaspoon white vinegar
- Pinch of salt and black pepper to taste
- Fresh chives or parsley, for garnish (optional)

Directions:

1. Start by toasting the whole-grain bread slices until they are golden and crisp. Set them aside on a plate.
2. Cut the ripe avocado in half and remove the pit. Scoop out the avocado flesh into a small bowl. Use a fork to mash the avocado until you achieve a smooth consistency. Season with a pinch of salt and black pepper to taste.
3. Fill a medium-sized saucepan with water and bring it to a gentle simmer over medium heat. Add the white vinegar to the water.
4. Carefully crack one egg into a small cup or ramekin. Create a gentle whirlpool in the simmering water by stirring it with a spoon, then slide the egg into the centre of the whirlpool. The swirling motion will help the egg white wrap around the yolk. For 3 to 4 minutes, poach the egg for a soft, runny yolk or longer if you prefer a firmer yolk. Remove the poached egg with a slotted spoon and place it on a plate lined with paper towels to drain any excess water. Repeat the process with the second egg.
5. Assemble the dish by spreading the mashed avocado evenly onto the toasted whole-grain bread slices.
6. Carefully place one poached egg on each slice of toast and avocado.
7. Garnish with fresh chives or parsley, if desired.
8. Serve immediately and enjoy!

Nutritional Information (per serving):

- Calories: 225 kcal
- Carbohydrates: 19g
- Protein: 10g
- Fat: 13g
- Saturated Fat: 2g
- Fibre: 8g
- Sugar: 1g
- Sodium: 150mg

2.GREEK YOGURT WITH BERRIES AND NUTS

Servings: 2
Prep time: 5 minutes

Ingredients:

- 240ml Greek yoghurt (low-fat or plain)
- 125g mixed berries (e.g., strawberries, blueberries, raspberries)
- 2 tablespoons chopped mixed nuts (e.g., almonds, walnuts, pistachios)
- 1 teaspoon honey or sugar-free sweetener (optional)
- Fresh mint leaves, for garnish (optional)

Directions:

1. In a medium-sized bowl, add the Greek yoghurt and stir it gently to ensure a smooth consistency.
2. Wash the mixed berries thoroughly and pat them dry with a paper towel. If using strawberries, remove the stems and slice them into bite-sized pieces.
3. Add the mixed berries to the Greek yoghurt and gently fold them in, ensuring an even distribution of fruit throughout the yoghurt.
4. If you prefer a touch of sweetness, drizzle 1 teaspoon of honey over the yoghurt and berries. Alternatively, use a sugar-free sweetener according to your preference.
5. Sprinkle the chopped mixed nuts over the top of the yoghurt and berries, adding a satisfying crunch and extra nutrients to the dish.
6. Garnish with fresh mint leaves for an added touch of freshness if desired.
7. Serve immediately and enjoy your diabetic-friendly Greek Yogurt with Berries and Nuts.

Nutritional Information (per serving):

- Calories: 150 kcal
- Carbohydrates: 15g
- Protein: 12g
- Fat: 6g
- Saturated Fat: 1g
- Fibre: 3g
- Sugar: 9g
- Sodium: 35mg

3. VEGGIE OMELETTE

Servings: 1
Prep time: 10 minutes
Cooking time: 10 minutes

Ingredients:

- 2 large eggs
- 2 tablespoons chopped onions
- 2 tablespoons chopped bell peppers (any colour)
- 2 tablespoons chopped tomatoes
- 75g chopped spinach or other leafy greens
- 1 tablespoon olive oil
- Pinch of salt and black pepper to taste
- Fresh herbs (e.g., parsley or chives), for garnish (optional)

Directions:

1. In a small bowl, whisk the eggs until well beaten. Season with a pinch of salt and black pepper to taste.
2. Heat the olive oil in a non-stick frying pan over medium heat.
3. Add the chopped onions and bell peppers to the pan. Sauté for 2-3 minutes until they become soft and slightly caramelised.
4. Add the chopped tomatoes and spinach (or other leafy greens) to the pan. Cook for another 1-2 minutes until the greens wilt, and the tomatoes are tender.
5. Pour the beaten eggs over the sautéed vegetables in the pan, spreading them out evenly to cover the entire surface.
6. Allow the omelette to cook for about 3-4 minutes or until the edges are set, and the centre is mostly cooked.
7. Gently fold the omelette in half using a spatula. Press down lightly to seal the edges.
8. Cook the folded omelette for another 1-2 minutes until it is fully set and cooked.
9. Slide the cooked omelette onto a plate and garnish with fresh herbs, if desired.
10. Serve the Diabetic Veggie Omelette hot, and enjoy a nutritious and delicious meal.

Nutritional Information (per serving):

- Calories: 220 kcal
- Carbohydrates: 6g
- Protein: 12g
- Fat: 16g
- Saturated Fat: 3g
- Fibre: 2g
- Sugar: 3g
- Sodium: 180mg

4. CHIA SEED PUDDING

Servings: 2
Prep time: 5 minutes
Chilling Time: 2 hours or overnight

Ingredients:

- 75g chia seeds
- 240ml unsweetened almond milk or coconut milk
- 1 teaspoon sugar-free sweetener (e.g., stevia, erythritol)
- 1/2 teaspoon vanilla extract
- Fresh berries or sliced fruits for topping
- Chopped nuts or seeds for topping (optional)

Directions:

1. In a mixing bowl, combine the chia seeds, unsweetened almond milk (or coconut milk), sugar-free sweetener, and vanilla extract. Stir well to ensure the chia seeds are evenly distributed in the liquid.
2. Cover the bowl with plastic wrap or a lid and refrigerate for at least 2 hours or overnight. The chia seeds will absorb the liquid and thicken to create a pudding-like consistency.
3. After the chilling time, give the chia seed mixture a good stir to break up any clumps and ensure a smooth texture.
4. Divide the Chia Seed Pudding into two serving bowls or glasses.
5. Top the pudding with fresh berries or sliced fruits of your choice. You can also add a sprinkle of chopped nuts or seeds for added crunch and flavour if desired.
6. Serve the Diabetic Chia Seed Pudding chilled, and enjoy a healthy and satisfying dessert or breakfast.

Nutritional Information (per serving):

- Calories: 150 kcal
- Carbohydrates: 11g
- Protein: 5g
- Fat: 10g
- Saturated Fat: 1g
- Fibre: 8g
- Sugar: 1g
- Sodium: 80mg

5. COTTAGE CHEESE WITH FLAXSEEDS AND CINNAMON

Servings: 1 serving
Prep time: 5 minutes

Ingredients:

- 125g low-fat cottage cheese
- 1 tablespoon ground flaxseeds
- 1/2 teaspoon ground cinnamon
- 1 teaspoon sugar-free sweetener (e.g., stevia, erythritol)
- Fresh berries or sliced fruits for topping (optional)

Directions:

1. Combine the low-fat cottage cheese, ground flaxseeds, and ground cinnamon in a small bowl. Mix well to ensure an even distribution of the ingredients.
2. If you prefer a touch of sweetness, add sugar-free sweetener to the mixture and stir until incorporated. Adjust the sweetness to your liking.
3. Transfer the Diabetic Cottage Cheese with Flaxseeds and Cinnamon to a serving bowl.
4. If desired, top the cottage cheese with fresh berries or sliced fruits. The natural sweetness of fruits complements the dish without added sugars.
5. Serve immediately and enjoy this nutritious and satisfying diabetic-friendly breakfast or snack.

Nutritional Information (per serving):

- Calories: 180 kcal
- Carbohydrates: 10g
- Protein: 15g
- Fat: 8g
- Saturated Fat: 2g
- Fibre: 4g
- Sugar: 3g
- Sodium: 300mg

6. BREAKFAST SMOOTHIE

Servings: 1 serving
Prep time: 5 minutes

Ingredients:

- 1/2 medium avocado, peeled and pitted
- 125g frozen berries (e.g., strawberries, blueberries, raspberries)
- 240ml unsweetened almond milk or coconut milk
- 1 tablespoon ground flaxseeds
- 1 teaspoon sugar-free sweetener (e.g., stevia, erythritol)
- 1/2 teaspoon vanilla extract
- 1/2 teaspoon ground cinnamon
- Ice cubes (optional)

Directions:

1. Combine the avocado, frozen berries, unsweetened almond milk (or coconut milk), ground flaxseeds, sugar-free sweetener, vanilla extract, and ground cinnamon.
2. Add a few ice cubes to the blender if you prefer a thicker consistency.
3. Blend all the ingredients until you achieve a smooth and creamy texture.
4. Taste the smoothie and adjust the sweetness or spices according to your preference.
5. Pour the Diabetic Breakfast Smoothie into a glass and serve immediately.

Nutritional Information (per serving):

- Calories: 250 kcal
- Carbohydrates: 18g
- Protein: 5g
- Fat: 18g
- Saturated Fat: 2g
- Fibre: 9g
- Sugar: 5g
- Sodium: 150mg

7. ALMOND FLOUR PANCAKES

Servings: 2 servings
Prep time: 10 minutes
Cooking time: 10 minutes

Ingredients:

- 250g almond flour
- 2 large eggs
- 60ml unsweetened almond milk or coconut milk
- 1 tablespoon sugar-free sweetener (e.g., stevia, erythritol)
- 1/2 teaspoon baking powder
- 1/2 teaspoon vanilla extract
- Pinch of salt
- Butter or oil for cooking
- Fresh berries or sugar-free syrup for topping (optional)

Directions:

1. Whisk together the almond flour, eggs, unsweetened almond milk (or coconut milk), sugar-free sweetener, baking powder, vanilla extract, and a pinch of salt. Mix until a smooth batter forms.
2. Allow the pancake batter to rest for 5 minutes to thicken slightly.
3. Preheat a non-stick frying pan or griddle over medium-low heat. Add a small amount of butter or oil to coat the surface.
4. Spoon about 60ml of the pancake batter onto the pan for each pancake. Spread the batter slightly to form a round shape.
5. Cook the pancakes on one side for 2-3 minutes until bubbles form on the surface. Flip the pancakes carefully and cook for 2-3 minutes on the other side or until both sides are golden brown.
6. Transfer the cooked pancakes to a plate and keep them warm.
7. Repeat the process with the remaining batter until all the pancakes are cooked.
8. Serve the Diabetic Almond Flour Pancakes warm, topped with fresh berries or sugar-free syrup if desired.

Nutritional Information (per serving, without toppings):

- Calories: 250 kcal
- Carbohydrates: 8g
- Protein: 11g
- Fat: 21g
- Saturated Fat: 2g
- Fibre: 4g
- Sugar: 1g
- Sodium: 180mg

8. VEGETABLE FRITTATA

Servings: 4
Prep time: 15 minutes
Cooking time: 20 minutes

Ingredients:

- 1 tablespoon olive oil
- 125g diced onions
- 250g chopped mixed vegetables (e.g., bell peppers, zucchini, spinach)
- 6 large eggs
- 60ml unsweetened almond milk or coconut milk
- 75g grated low-fat cheese (e.g., cheddar, mozzarella)
- 1/2 teaspoon dried herbs (e.g., thyme, oregano)
- Pinch of salt and black pepper, to taste
- Fresh herbs (e.g., parsley or chives), for garnish (optional)

Directions:

1. Preheat the oven to 180°C (350°F).
2. Heat the olive oil over medium heat in a non-stick ovenproof frying pan.
3. Add the diced onions and cook for 2-3 minutes until they become soft and translucent.
4. Add the chopped mixed vegetables to the pan and sauté for 3-4 minutes until slightly tender. You can use a combination of your favourite vegetables or whatever is available.
5. In a separate bowl, whisk together the eggs, unsweetened almond milk (or coconut milk), grated low-fat cheese, dried herbs, salt, and black pepper.
6. Pour the egg mixture evenly over the sautéed vegetables in the frying pan.
7. Cook the frittata on the stovetop over low heat for 2-3 minutes, allowing the edges to set.
8. Transfer the frying pan to the preheated oven and bake the frittata for approximately 10-12 minutes or until the centre is set and the top is lightly golden.
9. Once cooked, remove the frittata from the oven and let it cool slightly.
10. Garnish the Diabetic Vegetable Frittata with fresh herbs, if desired.
11. Slice the frittata into wedges and serve warm.

Nutritional Information (per serving):

- Calories: 180 kcal
- Carbohydrates: 6g
- Protein: 12g
- Fat: 12g
- Saturated Fat: 3g
- Fibre: 2g
- Sugar: 3g
- Sodium: 200mg

9. QUINOA BREAKFAST BOWL

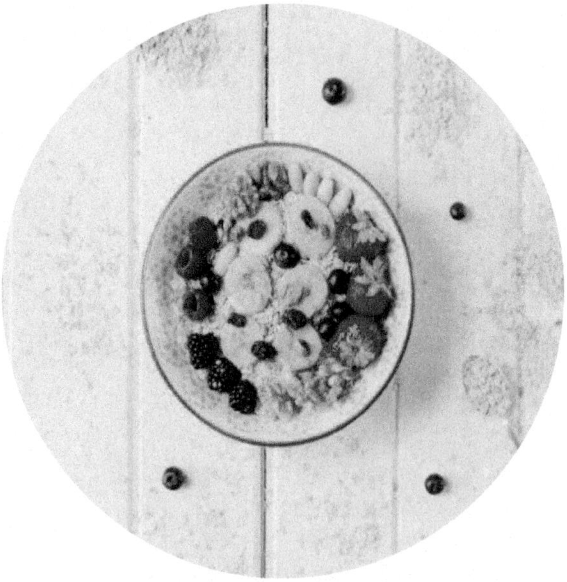

Servings: 2
Prep time: 10 minutes
Cooking time: 15 minutes

Ingredients:

- 125g quinoa
- 240ml unsweetened almond milk or coconut milk
- 1/2 teaspoon ground cinnamon
- 1/4 teaspoon vanilla extract
- 1 tablespoon chopped nuts (e.g., almonds, walnuts)
- 1 tablespoon ground flaxseeds
- Fresh berries or sliced fruits for topping
- Sugar-free sweetener (e.g., stevia, erythritol) or 1 tablespoon honey (optional)

Directions:

1. Rinse the quinoa under cold running water to remove any bitterness.
2. In a saucepan, combine the rinsed quinoa, unsweetened almond milk (or coconut milk), ground cinnamon, and vanilla extract.
3. Bring the mixture to a boil over medium-high heat, then reduce the heat to low and cover the saucepan with a lid. Simmer for 12-15 minutes or until the quinoa is cooked and the liquid is absorbed.
4. Once the quinoa is cooked, fluff it with a fork.
5. Divide the cooked quinoa into two serving bowls.
6. Top each bowl with chopped nuts, ground flaxseeds, and fresh berries or sliced fruits of your choice.
7. If desired, drizzle sugar-free sweetener or honey over the Quinoa Breakfast Bowl for added sweetness.
8. Serve the Diabetic Quinoa Breakfast Bowl warm and enjoy a wholesome and filling breakfast.

Nutritional Information (per serving, without sweetener):

- Calories: 200 kcal
- Carbohydrates: 26g
- Protein: 8g
- Fat: 8g
- Saturated Fat: 1g
- Fibre: 6g
- Sugar: 2g
- Sodium: 100mg

10. ALMOND BUTTER AND BERRIES OATMEAL

Servings: 2
Prep time: 5 minutes
Cooking time: 10 minutes

Ingredients:

- 250g rolled oats
- 240ml unsweetened almond milk or coconut milk
- 2 tablespoons almond butter
- 100g mixed berries (e.g., strawberries, blueberries, raspberries)
- 1 tablespoon ground flaxseeds
- 1/2 teaspoon ground cinnamon
- 1 teaspoon sugar-free sweetener (e.g., stevia, erythritol)
- Pinch of salt

Directions:

1. In a saucepan, combine the rolled oats, unsweetened almond milk (or coconut milk), almond butter, ground flaxseeds, ground cinnamon, sugar-free sweetener, and a pinch of salt.
2. Stir the mixture well to combine all the ingredients.
3. Place the saucepan over medium heat and bring the oatmeal to a gentle simmer.
4. Cook the oatmeal for about 8-10 minutes, stirring occasionally, until it reaches your desired thickness and creaminess.
5. Once the oatmeal is cooked, remove the saucepan from the heat.
6. Divide the Diabetic Almond Butter and Berries Oatmeal into two serving bowls.
7. Top each bowl with a generous amount of mixed berries.
8. If desired, drizzle sugar-free sweetener or honey over the oatmeal for added sweetness.
9. Serve the oatmeal warm, and enjoy a wholesome and delicious breakfast.

Nutritional Information (per serving):

- Calories: 300 kcal
- Carbohydrates: 35g
- Protein: 9g
- Fat: 15g
- Saturated Fat: 2g
- Fibre: 8g
- Sugar: 5g
- Sodium: 150mg

11. CINNAMON AND APPLE PORRIDGE

Servings: 2
Prep time: 5 minutes
Cooking time: 10 minutes

Ingredients:

- 250g rolled oats
- 240ml unsweetened almond milk or coconut milk
- 1 apple, peeled, cored, and diced
- 1/2 teaspoon ground cinnamon
- 1 tablespoon ground flaxseeds
- 1 teaspoon sugar-free sweetener (e.g., stevia, erythritol)
- Pinch of salt

Directions:

1. In a saucepan, combine the rolled oats, unsweetened almond milk (or coconut milk), diced apple, ground cinnamon, ground flaxseeds, sugar-free sweetener, and a pinch of salt.
2. Stir the mixture well to combine all the ingredients.
3. Place the saucepan over medium heat and bring the porridge to a gentle simmer.
4. Cook the porridge for about 8-10 minutes, stirring occasionally, until the oats are cooked and the apples are soft and tender.
5. Once the porridge is cooked, remove the saucepan from the heat.
6. Divide the Diabetic Cinnamon and Apple Porridge into two serving bowls.
7. If desired, drizzle sugar-free sweetener or honey over the porridge for added sweetness.
8. Serve the porridge warm and enjoy a comforting and delicious breakfast.

Nutritional Information (per serving, without sweetener):

- Calories: 250 kcal
- Carbohydrates: 35g
- Protein: 8g
- Fat: 9g
- Saturated Fat: 1g
- Fibre: 7g
- Sugar: 6g
- Sodium: 150mg

12. COCONUT MILK AND PINEAPPLE OATMEAL

Servings: 2
Prep time: 5 minutes
Cooking time: 10 minutes

Ingredients:

- 250g rolled oats
- 240ml unsweetened coconut milk
- 250g diced fresh pineapple
- 2 tablespoons unsweetened shredded coconut
- 1 tablespoon ground flaxseeds
- 1 teaspoon sugar-free sweetener (e.g., stevia, erythritol)
- Pinch of salt

Directions:

1. In a saucepan, combine the rolled oats, unsweetened coconut milk, diced fresh pineapple, unsweetened shredded coconut, ground flaxseeds, sugar-free sweetener, and a pinch of salt.
2. Stir the mixture well to combine all the ingredients.
3. Place the saucepan over medium heat and bring the oatmeal to a gentle simmer.
4. Cook the oatmeal for about 8-10 minutes, stirring occasionally, until the oats are cooked and the pineapple is soft and slightly caramelised.
5. Once the oatmeal is cooked, remove the saucepan from the heat.
6. Divide the Diabetic Coconut Milk and Pineapple Oatmeal into two serving bowls.
7. If desired, drizzle sugar-free sweetener or honey over the oatmeal for added sweetness.
8. Serve the oatmeal warm and enjoy a tropical and delicious breakfast.

Nutritional Information (per serving, without sweetener):

- Calories: 250 kcal
- Carbohydrates: 35g
- Protein: 7g
- Fat: 10g
- Saturated Fat: 7g
- Fibre: 7g
- Sugar: 8g
- Sodium: 50mg

13. PUMPKIN SPICE PORRIDGE

Servings: 2
Prep time: 5 minutes
Cooking time: 15 minutes

Ingredients:

- 250g rolled oats
- 480ml water
- 120ml pumpkin puree (unsweetened)
- 1/2 teaspoon ground cinnamon
- 1/4 teaspoon ground nutmeg
- 1/4 teaspoon ground ginger
- 1/4 teaspoon ground cloves
- 1 tablespoon ground flaxseeds
- 1 teaspoon sugar-free sweetener (e.g., stevia, erythritol)
- Chopped nuts or seeds for topping (e.g., walnuts, pumpkin seeds)
- Unsweetened almond milk or coconut milk, for drizzling (optional)

Directions:

1. In a saucepan, bring the water to a boil over medium heat.
2. Add the rolled oats to the boiling water and reduce the heat to low. Cook the oats for 5-7 minutes, stirring occasionally, until they reach your desired consistency.
3. Stir in the pumpkin puree, ground cinnamon, ground nutmeg, ground ginger, and ground cloves. Continue cooking for an additional 3-5 minutes to allow the flavours to meld together.
4. Remove the saucepan from the heat once the porridge is cooked and has thickened.
5. Stir in the ground flaxseeds and sugar-free sweetener to enhance the nutritional value and sweetness of the porridge.
6. Divide the Diabetic Pumpkin Spice Porridge into two serving bowls.
7. Top each bowl with chopped nuts or seeds for added crunch and nutrients.
8. If desired, drizzle unsweetened almond milk or coconut milk over the porridge for a creamy finish.
9. Serve the porridge warm and enjoy a comforting and spiced breakfast.

Nutritional Information (per serving, without sweetener):

- Calories: 250 kcal
- Carbohydrates: 35g
- Protein: 8g
- Fat: 10g
- Saturated Fat: 1g
- Fibre: 8g
- Sugar: 2g
- Sodium: 10mg

14. NUTTY QUINOA PORRIDGE

Servings: 2
Prep time: 5 minutes
Cooking time: 20 minutes

Ingredients:

- 125g quinoa
- 240ml water
- 240ml unsweetened almond milk or coconut milk
- 2 tablespoons chopped mixed nuts (e.g., almonds, walnuts, pistachios)
- 1 tablespoon ground flaxseeds
- 1 teaspoon sugar-free sweetener (e.g., stevia, erythritol)
- 1/2 teaspoon ground cinnamon
- Pinch of salt
- Fresh fruits (e.g., berries, sliced banana), for topping

Directions:

1. Rinse the quinoa under cold running water to remove any bitterness.
2. In a saucepan, combine the rinsed quinoa and water. Bring the quinoa to a boil over medium heat.
3. Reduce the heat to low, cover the saucepan with a lid, and let the quinoa simmer for about 12-15 minutes or until all the water is absorbed and the quinoa is cooked and fluffy.
4. Stir in the unsweetened almond milk (or coconut milk) and continue cooking for another 5 minutes, or until the porridge reaches your desired consistency.
5. Add the chopped mixed nuts, ground flaxseeds, sugar-free sweetener, ground cinnamon, and a pinch of salt. Mix well to combine all the ingredients.
6. Divide the Diabetic Nutty Quinoa Porridge into two serving bowls.
7. Top each bowl with fresh fruits for added sweetness and nutrients.
8. Serve the porridge warm and enjoy a wholesome and nutty breakfast.

Nutritional Information (per serving, without sweetener):

- Calories: 250 kcal
- Carbohydrates: 30g
- Protein: 10g
- Fat: 10g
- Saturated Fat: 1g
- Fibre: 5g
- Sugar: 2g
- Sodium: 150mg

15. CHOCOLATE PROTEIN OATS

Servings: 2
Prep time: 5 minutes
Cooking time: 10 minutes

Ingredients:

- 250g rolled oats
- 480ml water
- 2 tablespoons unsweetened cocoa powder
- 2 tablespoons chocolate protein powder (sugar-free)
- 1 tablespoon ground flaxseeds
- 1 teaspoon sugar-free sweetener (e.g., stevia, erythritol)
- Pinch of salt
- Fresh berries or sliced fruits, for topping

Directions:

1. In a saucepan, bring the water to a boil over medium heat.
2. Add the rolled oats to the boiling water and reduce the heat to low. Cook the oats for 5-7 minutes, stirring occasionally, until they reach your desired consistency.
3. Stir in the unsweetened cocoa powder and chocolate protein powder. Continue cooking for 2-3 minutes to infuse the oats with chocolate flavour and protein.
4. Add the ground flaxseeds, sugar-free sweetener, and a pinch of salt. Mix well to combine all the ingredients.
5. Divide the Diabetic Chocolate Protein Oats into two serving bowls.
6. Top each bowl with fresh berries or sliced fruits for sweetness and nutrients.
7. Serve the oats warm and enjoy a delicious and protein-packed breakfast.

Nutritional Information (per serving, without sweetener):

- Calories: 250 kcal
- Carbohydrates: 30g
- Protein: 12g
- Fat: 7g
- Saturated Fat: 1g
- Fibre: 6g
- Sugar: 1g
- Sodium: 50mg

16. COCONUT AND MANGO OATMEAL

Servings: 2
Prep time: 5 minutes
Cooking time: 10 minutes

Ingredients:

- 250g rolled oats
- 480ml water
- 100ml unsweetened coconut milk
- 1 ripe mango, peeled and diced
- 2 tablespoons unsweetened shredded coconut
- 1 tablespoon ground flaxseeds
- 1/2 teaspoon ground cinnamon
- Pinch of salt

Directions:

1. In a saucepan, bring the water to a boil over medium heat.
2. Add the rolled oats to the boiling water and reduce the heat to low. Cook the oats for 5-7 minutes, stirring occasionally, until they reach your desired consistency.
3. Stir in the unsweetened coconut milk, diced mango, unsweetened shredded coconut, ground flaxseeds, ground cinnamon, and a pinch of salt. Continue cooking for 2-3 minutes to infuse the oats with coconut and mango flavours.
4. Remove the saucepan from the heat once the oatmeal is cooked and has thickened.
5. Divide the Diabetic Coconut and Mango Oatmeal into two serving bowls.
6. Serve the oatmeal warm and enjoy a tropical and delicious breakfast.

Nutritional Information (per serving):

- Calories: 250 kcal
- Carbohydrates: 35g
- Protein: 6g
- Fat: 10g
- Saturated Fat: 7g
- Fibre: 6g
- Sugar: 12g
- Sodium: 50mg

17. LEMON BLUEBERRY CHIA PORRIDGE

Servings: 2
Prep time: 5 minutes
Cooking time: 10 minutes

Ingredients:

- 250g rolled oats
- 480ml water
- Zest of 1 lemon
- 1 tablespoon chia seeds
- 125g fresh blueberries
- 1 tablespoon ground flaxseeds
- 1/2 teaspoon vanilla extract
- Pinch of salt

Directions:

1. In a saucepan, bring the water to a boil over medium heat.
2. Add the rolled oats to the boiling water and reduce the heat to low. Cook the oats for about 5-7 minutes, stirring occasionally, until they reach your desired consistency.
3. Stir in the lemon zest, chia seeds, fresh blueberries, ground flaxseeds, vanilla extract, and a pinch of salt. Continue cooking for another 2-3 minutes to infuse the oats with lemon and blueberry flavours.
4. Once the porridge is cooked and has thickened, remove the saucepan from the heat.
5. Divide the Diabetic Lemon Blueberry Chia Porridge into two serving bowls.
6. Serve the porridge warm and enjoy a refreshing and nutritious breakfast.

Nutritional Information (per serving):

- Calories: 200 kcal
- Carbohydrates: 30g
- Protein: 6g
- Fat: 7g
- Saturated Fat: 1g
- Fibre: 6g
- Sugar: 5g
- Sodium: 50mg

18. PECAN PIE OATMEAL

Servings: 2
Prep time: 5 minutes
Cooking time: 10 minutes

Ingredients:

- 250g rolled oats
- 250g water
- 2 tablespoons chopped pecans
- 1 tablespoon ground flaxseeds
- 1/2 teaspoon ground cinnamon
- 1/4 teaspoon vanilla extract
- 1/4 teaspoon almond extract (optional)
- Pinch of salt
- Sugar-free sweetener (e.g., stevia, erythritol) to taste (optional)

Directions:

1. In a saucepan, bring the water to a boil over medium heat.
2. Add the rolled oats to the boiling water and reduce the heat to low. Cook the oats for 5-7 minutes, stirring occasionally, until they reach your desired consistency.
3. Stir in the chopped pecans, flaxseeds, cinnamon, vanilla extract, almond extract (if using), and a pinch of salt. Continue cooking for 2-3 minutes to infuse the oats with pecan pie flavours.
4. Remove the saucepan from the heat once the oatmeal is cooked and has thickened.
5. Divide the Diabetic Pecan Pie Oatmeal into two serving bowls.
6. If desired, add sugar-free sweetener to taste for added sweetness.
7. Serve the oatmeal warm and enjoy a delicious and indulgent breakfast.

Nutritional Information (per serving, without sweetener):

- Calories: 250 kcal
- Carbohydrates: 30g
- Protein: 7g
- Fat: 10g
- Saturated Fat: 1g
- Fibre: 6g
- Sugar: 1g
- Sodium: 50mg

19.GINGER AND PEAR PORRIDGE

Servings: 2
Prep time: 5 minutes
Cooking time: 10 minutes

Ingredients:

- 250g rolled oats
- 480ml water
- 1 ripe pear, peeled, cored, and diced
- 1 tablespoon fresh ginger, grated
- 1 tablespoon ground flaxseeds
- 1/2 teaspoon ground cinnamon
- Pinch of salt

Directions:

1. In a saucepan, bring the water to a boil over medium heat.
2. Add the rolled oats to the boiling water and reduce the heat to low. Cook the oats for 5-7 minutes, stirring occasionally, until they reach your desired consistency.
3. Stir in the diced pear, grated ginger, flaxseeds, cinnamon, and a pinch of salt. Continue cooking for another 2-3 minutes to infuse the oats with ginger and pear flavours.
4. Once the porridge is cooked and has thickened, remove the saucepan from the heat.
5. Divide the Diabetic Ginger and Pear Porridge into two serving bowls.
6. Serve the porridge warm and enjoy a delicious and fruity breakfast.

Nutritional Information (per serving):

- Calories: 200 kcal
- Carbohydrates: 35g
- Protein: 6g
- Fat: 5g
- Saturated Fat: 1g
- Fibre: 6g
- Sugar: 7g
- Sodium: 50mg

20. RASPBERRY AND ALMOND PORRIDGE

Servings: 2
Prep time: 5 minutes
Cooking time: 10 minutes

Ingredients:

- 250g rolled oats
- 480ml water
- 250g fresh raspberries
- 2 tablespoons almond butter
- 2 tablespoons unsweetened almond milk
- 1 tablespoon ground flaxseeds
- 1/2 teaspoon almond extract
- Pinch of salt

Directions:

1. In a saucepan, bring the water to a boil over medium heat.
2. Add the rolled oats to the boiling water and reduce the heat to low. Cook the oats for 5-7 minutes, stirring occasionally, until they reach your desired consistency.
3. Stir in the fresh raspberries, almond butter, unsweetened almond milk, ground flaxseeds, almond extract, and a pinch of salt. Continue cooking for another 2-3 minutes to infuse the oats with raspberry and almond flavours.
4. Remove the saucepan from the heat once the porridge is cooked and has thickened.
5. Divide the Diabetic Raspberry and Almond Porridge into two serving bowls.
6. Serve the porridge warm and enjoy a delicious and fruity breakfast.

Nutritional Information (per serving):

- Calories: 250 kcal
- Carbohydrates: 35g
- Protein: 8g
- Fat: 10g
- Saturated Fat: 1g
- Fibre: 7g
- Sugar: 5g
- Sodium: 50mg

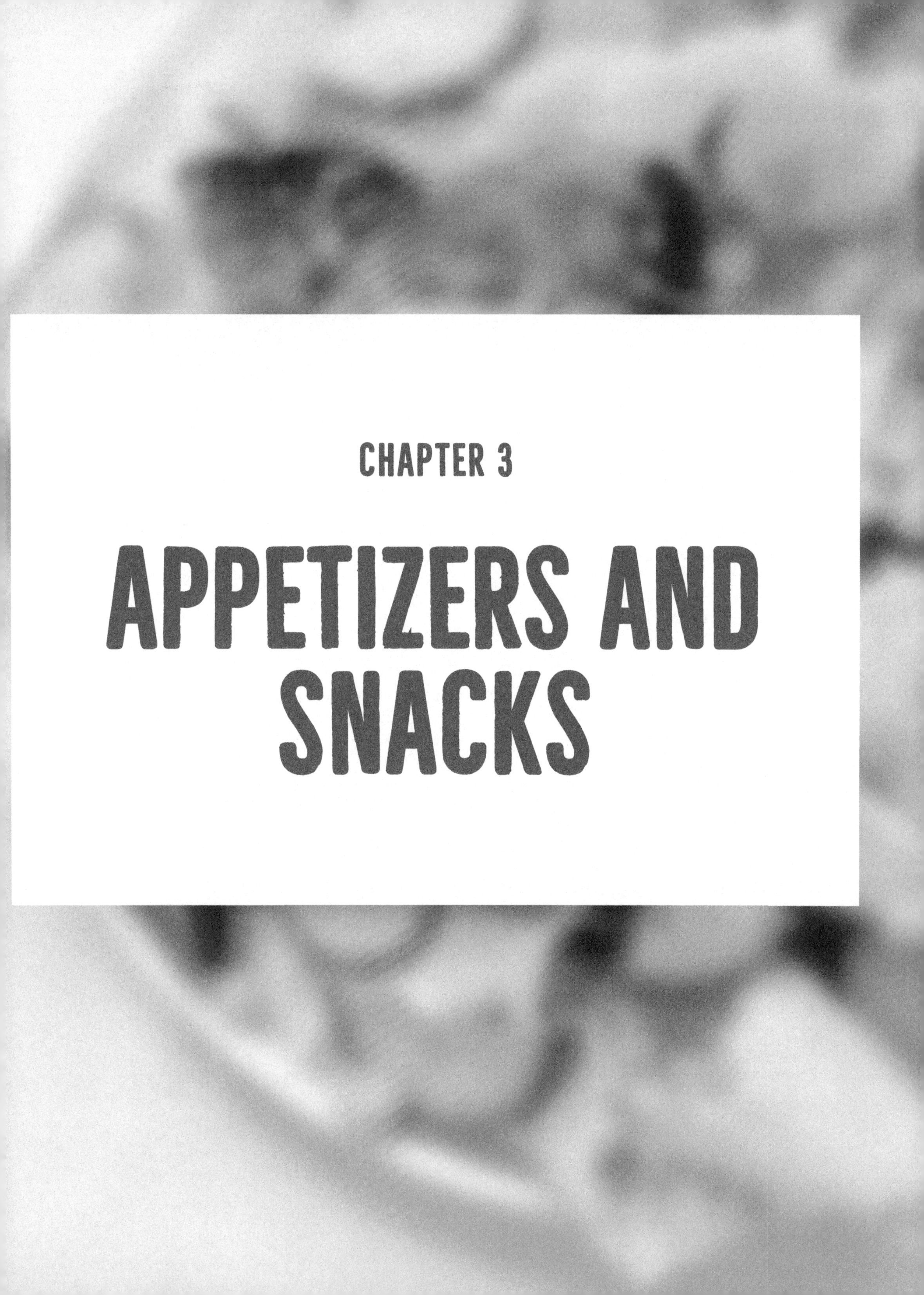

CHAPTER 3

APPETIZERS AND SNACKS

1. VEGGIE STICKS WITH HUMMUS

Servings: 4
Prep time: 15 minutes
Cooking time: 0 minutes

Ingredients: For Hummus:

- 1 can (400g) chickpeas, drained and rinsed
- 2 garlic cloves, minced
- 3 tablespoons tahini
- 3 tablespoons lemon juice
- 2 tablespoons water
- 2 tablespoons olive oil
- 1/2 teaspoon ground cumin
- Salt and pepper to taste

For Veggie Sticks:

- 2 large carrots, peeled and cut into sticks
- 2 large cucumbers, cut into sticks
- 2 bell peppers (assorted colors), cut into sticks
- 1 celery stalk, cut into sticks

Directions:

1. In a food processor, combine the drained chickpeas, minced garlic, tahini, lemon juice, water, olive oil, ground cumin, salt, and pepper.
2. Blend the ingredients until you achieve a smooth and creamy consistency. If needed, adjust the seasonings to suit your taste.
3. Transfer the hummus to a serving bowl and refrigerate until ready to serve.
4. Prepare the vegetable sticks by cutting the carrots, cucumbers, bell peppers, and celery into sticks.
5. Arrange the veggie sticks on a serving platter.
6. Serve the Diabetic Veggie Sticks with Hummus and enjoy this healthy and delicious snack.

Nutritional Information (per serving - 1/4 of the hummus and veggie sticks):

- Calories: 180 kcal
- Carbohydrates: 22g
- Protein: 7g
- Fat: 9g
- Saturated Fat: 1g
- Fibre: 6g
- Sugar: 4g
- Sodium: 220mg

2. GUACAMOLE WITH BELL PEPPER SLICES

Servings: 4
Prep time: 15 minutes
Cooking time: 0 minutes

Ingredients:

- 2 ripe avocados
- 1 small red onion, finely diced
- 1 small tomato, diced and seeds removed
- 1 jalapeno pepper, finely chopped (optional for heat)
- 2 cloves garlic, minced
- 1 lime, juiced
- 75g chopped fresh cilantro
- Salt and pepper to taste
- 2 large bell peppers (assorted colours), sliced for serving

Directions:

1. Cut the avocados in half, remove the pits, and scoop the flesh into a mixing bowl.
2. Use a fork to mash the avocado until you achieve your desired guacamole consistency (smooth or chunky).
3. Add the finely diced red onion, tomato, chopped jalapeno pepper (if using), minced garlic, lime juice, and chopped cilantro to the bowl.
4. Mix all the ingredients until well combined.
5. Season the guacamole with salt and pepper to taste.
6. Transfer the Diabetic Guacamole to a serving bowl and refrigerate until ready to serve.
7. Prepare the bell peppers by slicing them into sticks.
8. Arrange the bell pepper slices on a serving platter.
9. Serve the Diabetic Guacamole with bell pepper slices, and enjoy this delicious and healthy snack.

Nutritional Information (per serving - 1/4 of the guacamole and bell pepper slices):

- Calories: 150 kcal
- Carbohydrates: 12g
- Protein: 2g
- Fat: 11g
- Saturated Fat: 2g
- Fibre: 7g
- Sugar: 2g
- Sodium: 10mg

3. DEVILED EGGS

Servings: 12
Prep time: 15 minutes
Cooking time: 10 minutes

Ingredients:

- 6 large eggs
- 2 tablespoons plain Greek yoghurt
- 1 tablespoon Dijon mustard
- 1 teaspoon white vinegar
- 1/2 teaspoon garlic powder
- 1/2 teaspoon onion powder
- Salt and pepper to taste
- Paprika and fresh parsley, for garnish (optional)

Directions:

1. Place the eggs in a single layer in a saucepan and cover them with water.
2. Bring the water to a boil over medium-high heat, then reduce the heat to low and let the eggs simmer for about 10 minutes.
3. Remove the saucepan from the heat and transfer the eggs to a bowl of ice water to cool for a few minutes.
4. Once the eggs are cool, carefully peel off the shells and slice them in half lengthwise.
5. Gently scoop the yolks from the eggs and place them in a separate bowl.
6. Mash the egg yolks with a fork until they become crumbly.
7. Add the plain Greek yoghurt, Dijon mustard, white vinegar, garlic powder, onion powder, salt, and pepper to the bowl with the egg yolks.
8. Mix all the ingredients until well combined and smooth.
9. Spoon the deviled egg filling into the halved egg whites, dividing it evenly among them.
10. Garnish the Deviled Eggs with a sprinkle of paprika and some fresh parsley if desired.
11. Refrigerate the Deviled Eggs until ready to serve.
12. Serve the Diabetic Deviled Eggs as a tasty and healthy appetiser or snack.

Nutritional Information (per serving - 1 deviled egg):

- Calories: 50 kcal
- Carbohydrates: 1g
- Protein: 4g
- Fat: 3.5g
- Saturated Fat: 1g
- Fibre: 0g
- Sugar: 0g
- Sodium: 70mg

4. CAPRESE SALAD SKEWERS

Servings: 12 skewers
Prep time: 20 minutes
Cooking time: 0 minutes

Ingredients:

- 24 cherry tomatoes
- 12 small fresh mozzarella balls
- 12 fresh basil leaves
- 2 tablespoons extra-virgin olive oil
- 2 tablespoons balsamic vinegar
- Salt and pepper to taste
- Wooden skewers or toothpicks

Directions:

1. Wash the cherry tomatoes and pat them dry. Wash the fresh basil leaves and gently dry them with a paper towel.
2. On each wooden skewer or toothpick, thread a cherry tomato, followed by a fresh basil leaf, and then a small fresh mozzarella ball. Repeat this pattern for all 12 skewers.
3. Arrange the Caprese Salad Skewers on a serving platter.
4. Mix the extra-virgin olive oil and balsamic vinegar to make the dressing.
5. Drizzle the dressing over the Caprese Salad Skewers.
6. Season the skewers with a sprinkle of salt and pepper to taste.
7. Serve the Diabetic Caprese Salad Skewers as a delightful and refreshing appetiser or snack.

Nutritional Information (per skewer):

- Calories: 50 kcal
- Carbohydrates: 1g
- Protein: 3g
- Fat: 4g
- Saturated Fat: 2g
- Fibre: 0g
- Sugar: 0g
- Sodium: 50mg

5. MIXED NUTS

Servings: 10
Prep time: 5 minutes
Cooking time: 10 minutes

Ingredients:

- 500g mixed nuts (e.g., almonds, walnuts, cashews, peanuts, pecans)
- 1 tablespoon olive oil
- 1/2 teaspoon ground cumin
- 1/2 teaspoon paprika
- 1/4 teaspoon garlic powder
- 1/4 teaspoon onion powder
- 1/4 teaspoon cayenne pepper (optional, for heat)
- Salt to taste

Directions:

1. Preheat the oven to 180°C (350°F).
2. In a mixing bowl, combine the mixed nuts with olive oil, ground cumin, paprika, garlic powder, onion powder, cayenne pepper (if using), and salt.
3. Toss the nuts until they are evenly coated with the seasoning.
4. Spread the seasoned nuts in a single layer on a baking sheet lined with parchment paper.
5. Roast the nuts in the preheated oven for about 10 minutes, or until they become fragrant and slightly toasted. Stir the nuts halfway through the cooking time to ensure even roasting.
6. Remove the baking sheet from the oven and let the nuts cool completely.
7. Once the nuts are cooled, transfer them to an airtight container for storage.
8. Serve the Diabetic Mixed Nuts as a delicious and healthy snack.

Nutritional Information (per serving - 1/4 cup):

- Calories: 150 kcal
- Carbohydrates: 5g
- Protein: 5g
- Fat: 13g
- Saturated Fat: 2g
- Fibre: 2g
- Sugar: 1g
- Sodium: 50mg

6. CHEESE PLATTER

Servings: 6
Prep time: 15 minutes

Ingredients:

- 200g hard cheese (e.g., cheddar, gouda, or Swiss), cubed or sliced
- 200g soft cheese (e.g., brie, camembert, or goat cheese), cut into wedges
- 250g mixed nuts (e.g., almonds, walnuts, cashews)
- 250g fresh berries (e.g., strawberries, blueberries, raspberries)
- 250g cherry tomatoes
- 250g sliced cucumber
- 125g sliced bell peppers (assorted colours)
- 125g olives (assorted varieties)
- 1 tablespoon sugar-free jam or chutney (optional)
- Fresh herbs (e.g., basil, thyme) for garnish

Directions:

1. Arrange the hard cheese and soft cheese on a serving platter, leaving space for other ingredients.
2. Place the mixed nuts in a separate bowl or small dish and position it on the platter.
3. Arrange the fresh berries, cherry tomatoes, sliced cucumber, and bell peppers on the platter between the cheese.
4. Add the olives to the platter, distributing them evenly.
5. If using sugar-free jam or chutney, place it in a small bowl on the platter.
6. Garnish the cheese platter with fresh herbs for an attractive presentation.
7. Serve the Diabetic Cheese Platter with whole-grain crackers or vegetable sticks for a delightful and wholesome treat.

Nutritional Information (per serving):

- Calories: 250 kcal
- Carbohydrates: 8g
- Protein: 12g
- Fat: 20g
- Saturated Fat: 8g
- Fibre: 3g
- Sugar: 4g
- Sodium: 300mg

7.BAKED ZUCCHINI CHIPS

Servings: 4
Prep time: 15 minutes
Cooking time: 25 minutes

Ingredients:

- 2 medium zucchini, washed and sliced into thin rounds
- 2 tablespoons olive oil
- 75g grated Parmesan cheese
- 75g breadcrumbs (use whole-grain or almond flour for a low-carb option)
- 1/2 teaspoon garlic powder
- 1/2 teaspoon paprika
- Salt and pepper to taste
- Cooking spray (olive oil or vegetable oil spray)

Directions:

1. Preheat the oven to 200°C (390°F). Line a baking sheet with parchment paper and lightly coat it with cooking spray.
2. Combine the grated Parmesan cheese, breadcrumbs (or almond flour), garlic powder, paprika, salt, and pepper.
3. Toss the zucchini slices with olive oil, ensuring they are evenly coated.
4. Take each zucchini slice and dip it into the Parmesan-breadcrumb mixture, pressing gently to adhere the coating to both sides.
5. Place the coated zucchini slices in a single layer on the prepared baking sheet.
6. Lightly spray the top of the zucchini slices with cooking spray to help them crisp up while baking.
7. Bake the zucchini chips in the preheated oven for about 20-25 minutes, or until they become golden brown and crispy.
8. Remove the baking sheet from the oven and let the zucchini chips cool slightly before serving.
9. Serve the Diabetic Baked Zucchini Chips as a healthy and flavoursome snack.

Nutritional Information (per serving - approximately 1/4 of the zucchini chips):

- Calories: 120 kcal
- Carbohydrates: 8g
- Protein: 4g
- Fat: 8g
- Saturated Fat: 2g
- Fibre: 2g
- Sugar: 2g
- Sodium: 180mg

8. TUNA LETTUCE WRAPS

Servings: 4
Prep time: 15 minutes

Ingredients:

- 2 cans (200g each) tuna in water, drained
- 75g cucumber, diced
- 75g carrot, grated
- 75g red bell pepper, diced
- 2 tablespoons red onion, finely chopped
- 2 tablespoons fresh parsley, chopped
- 2 tablespoons olive oil
- 1 tablespoon lemon juice
- 1/2 teaspoon Dijon mustard
- Salt and pepper to taste
- 8 large lettuce leaves (e.g., romaine or butterhead)

Directions:

1. In a large bowl, combine the drained tuna, diced cucumber, grated carrot, diced red bell pepper, chopped red onion, and fresh parsley.
2. In a separate small bowl, whisk together the olive oil, lemon juice, Dijon mustard, salt, and pepper to make the dressing.
3. Pour the dressing over the tuna mixture and toss everything together until well coated.
4. Place a spoonful of the tuna mixture onto each lettuce leaf.
5. Wrap the lettuce around the tuna mixture to form a neat and compact wrap.
6. Repeat the process for all lettuce leaves and tuna mixture.
7. Serve the Diabetic Tuna Lettuce Wraps as a light and refreshing meal option.

Nutritional Information (per serving - 2 lettuce wraps):

- Calories: 250 kcal
- Carbohydrates: 7g
- Protein: 25g
- Fat: 14g
- Saturated Fat: 2g
- Fibre: 2g
- Sugar: 3g
- Sodium: 280mg

9. CUCUMBER CUPS WITH TZATZIKI

Servings: 4
Prep time: 20 minutes

Ingredients:

- 2 large cucumbers
- 250ml Greek yoghurt
- 125g grated cucumber (from one of the large cucumbers)
- 2 cloves garlic, minced
- 1 tablespoon fresh dill, chopped
- 1 tablespoon fresh mint, chopped
- 1 tablespoon lemon juice
- 1 tablespoon extra-virgin olive oil
- Salt and pepper to taste
- Cherry tomatoes and fresh dill for garnish (optional)

Directions:

1. Peel the cucumbers, leaving some thin strips of skin for aesthetics, if desired. Cut the cucumbers into 2-inch thick slices.
2. Use a melon baller or a teaspoon to carefully scoop out the centre of each cucumber slice, creating a cup-like shape. Make sure not to scoop all the way through the bottom.
3. Combine the Greek yoghurt, grated cucumber, minced garlic, chopped dill, chopped mint, lemon juice, extra-virgin olive oil, salt, and pepper in a bowl. Mix well to make the tzatziki sauce.
4. Fill each cucumber cup with the prepared tzatziki sauce using a spoon or a piping bag.
5. Garnish the Diabetic Cucumber Cups with Tzatziki with cherry tomatoes and fresh dill, if desired.
6. Serve the cucumber cups as a refreshing and tangy appetiser or snack.

Nutritional Information (per serving - 2 cucumber cups):

- Calories: 120 kcal
- Carbohydrates: 6g
- Protein: 6g
- Fat: 8g
- Saturated Fat: 2g
- Fibre: 1g
- Sugar: 4g
- Sodium: 60mg

10. ROASTED CHICKPEAS

Servings: 4
Prep time: 10 minutes
Cooking time: 25 minutes

Ingredients:

- 2 cans (400g each) chickpeas, drained and rinsed
- 2 tablespoons olive oil
- 1 teaspoon ground cumin
- 1/2 teaspoon ground coriander
- 1/2 teaspoon paprika
- 1/2 teaspoon garlic powder
- Salt and pepper to taste

Directions:

1. Preheat the oven to 200°C (390°F).
2. Pat the drained chickpeas dry with a paper towel to remove excess moisture.
3. In a mixing bowl, toss the chickpeas with olive oil until they are evenly coated.
4. Mix the ground cumin, coriander, paprika, garlic powder, salt, and pepper in a separate small bowl.
5. Sprinkle the spice mixture over the chickpeas and toss them again to ensure even seasoning.
6. Spread the seasoned chickpeas in a single layer on a baking sheet lined with parchment paper.
7. Roast the chickpeas in the oven for about 20-25 minutes or until they become crispy and slightly golden.
8. Remove the baking sheet from the oven and let the roasted chickpeas cool slightly before serving.
9. Serve the Diabetic Roasted Chickpeas as a crunchy and protein-packed snack.

Nutritional Information (per serving - approximately 1/2 cup):

- Calories: 200 kcal
- Carbohydrates: 20g
- Protein: 8g
- Fat: 8g
- Saturated Fat: 1g
- Fibre: 6g
- Sugar: 1g
- Sodium: 150mg

11. STUFFED MUSHROOMS

Servings: 4
Prep time: 20 minutes
Cooking time: 20 minutes

Ingredients:

- 8 large mushrooms (portobello or button mushrooms)
- 1 tablespoon olive oil
- 75g finely chopped onion
- 2 cloves garlic, minced
- 250g spinach, chopped
- 125g grated zucchini
- 75g grated Parmesan cheese
- 75g cream cheese (use reduced-fat cream cheese for a lighter option)
- 1/4 teaspoon dried thyme
- Salt and pepper to taste
- Fresh parsley for garnish (optional)

Directions:

1. Preheat the oven to 180°C (350°F).
2. Remove the stems from the mushrooms and finely chop them. Set the mushroom caps aside.
3. In a large skillet, heat the olive oil over medium heat.
4. Add the chopped mushroom stems, onion, and minced garlic to the skillet. Sauté until the onions are soft and translucent.
5. Stir in the chopped spinach and grated zucchini, cooking until the spinach wilts and any excess moisture evaporates.
6. Remove the skillet from the heat and let the mixture cool slightly.
7. Combine the sautéed vegetables in a bowl with grated Parmesan cheese, cream cheese, dried thyme, salt, and pepper. Mix everything until well combined.
8. Spoon the filling into each mushroom cap, pressing down gently to pack the filling.
9. Place the stuffed mushrooms on a baking sheet lined with parchment paper.
10. Bake the stuffed mushrooms in the preheated oven for about 15-20 minutes or until the mushrooms are tender and the filling is lightly browned.
11. Remove the baking sheet from the oven and let the stuffed mushrooms cool slightly before serving.
12. Garnish the Diabetic Stuffed Mushrooms with fresh parsley, if desired.
13. Serve the stuffed mushrooms as a delectable and savoury appetiser or side dish.

Nutritional Information (per serving - 2 stuffed mushrooms):

- Calories: 150 kcal
- Carbohydrates: 7g
- Protein: 8g
- Fat: 10g
- Saturated Fat: 4g
- Fibre: 2g
- Sugar: 3g
- Sodium: 230mg

12. BAKED PARMESAN ZUCCHINI FRIES

Servings: 4
Prep time: 15 minutes
Cooking time: 20 minutes

Ingredients:

- 2 large zucchini, washed and cut into fry-shaped strips
- 125g grated Parmesan cheese
- 125g breadcrumbs (use whole-grain or almond flour for a low-carb option)
- 1 teaspoon dried oregano
- 1 teaspoon garlic powder
- 1/2 teaspoon paprika
- 2 large eggs, beaten
- Cooking spray (olive oil or vegetable oil spray)
- Salt and pepper to taste
- Fresh parsley for garnish (optional)

Directions:

1. Preheat the oven to 220°C (425°F). Line a baking sheet with parchment paper and lightly coat it with cooking spray.
2. Combine the grated Parmesan cheese, breadcrumbs (or almond flour), dried oregano, garlic powder, paprika, salt, and pepper in a shallow dish.
3. Dip each zucchini strip into the beaten eggs, coating it thoroughly.
4. Next, roll the egg-coated zucchini strip in the Parmesan-breadcrumb mixture, pressing gently to adhere the coating to all sides.
5. Place the coated zucchini strips on the prepared baking sheet in a single layer, leaving space between them.
6. Lightly spray the top of the zucchini fries with cooking spray to help them crisp up while baking.
7. Bake the zucchini fries in the oven for about 18-20 minutes or until they become golden brown and crispy.
8. Remove the baking sheet from the oven and let the zucchini fries cool slightly before serving.
9. Garnish the Diabetic Baked Parmesan Zucchini Fries with fresh parsley, if desired.
10. Serve the zucchini fries as a delicious and diabetes-friendly appetiser or side dish.

Nutritional Information (per serving):

- Calories: 130 kcal
- Carbohydrates: 8g
- Protein: 9g
- Fat: 6g
- Saturated Fat: 3g
- Fibre: 2g
- Sugar: 2g
- Sodium: 240mg

13. EDAMAME WITH SEA SALT

Servings: 4
Prep time: 5 minutes
Cooking time: 5 minutes

Ingredients:

- 400g frozen edamame beans (shelled)
- 1 tablespoon sea salt

Directions:

1. In a large saucepan, bring water to a boil.
2. Add the frozen edamame beans to the boiling water and cook for about 5 minutes or until tender.
3. Drain the edamame beans and transfer them to a serving bowl.
4. Sprinkle the sea salt over the cooked edamame beans and toss them gently to ensure even seasoning.
5. Serve the Diabetic Edamame with Sea Salt as a delightful and nutritious snack or side dish.

Nutritional Information (per serving - approximately 100g):

- Calories: 110 kcal
- Carbohydrates: 8g
- Protein: 10g
- Fat: 4g
- Saturated Fat: 0.5g
- Fibre: 4g
- Sugar: 2g
- Sodium: 880mg

CHAPTER 4

MAIN COURSE (MEAT & FISH)

1. GRILLED CHICKEN BREAST WITH LEMON AND HERBS

Servings: 4
Prep time: 10 minutes
Cooking time: 15 minutes

Ingredients:

- 4 boneless, skinless chicken breasts (about 150g each)
- 2 tablespoons olive oil
- Zest of 1 lemon
- Juice of 1 lemon
- 2 cloves garlic, minced
- 1 teaspoon dried thyme
- 1 teaspoon dried rosemary
- Salt and pepper to taste
- Fresh parsley for garnish (optional)

Directions:

1. Combine the olive oil, lemon zest, lemon juice, minced garlic, dried thyme, rosemary, salt, and pepper to make the marinade.
2. Place the chicken breasts in a shallow dish and pour the marinade over them, ensuring they are evenly coated. Cover the dish with cling film and refrigerate for 30 minutes to marinate. For best results, marinate the chicken for several hours or overnight.
3. Preheat the grill to medium-high heat.
4. Remove the chicken breasts from the marinade, allowing any excess to drip off.
5. Place the chicken breasts on the grill and cook for about 6-7 minutes on each side or until they are cooked through and have grill marks.
6. Remove the grilled chicken breasts from the grill and let them rest for a few minutes before serving.
7. Garnish the Diabetic Grilled Chicken Breast with Lemon and Herbs with fresh parsley, if desired.
8. Serve the grilled chicken breasts as a delicious and protein-packed main course.

Nutritional Information (per serving - 1 chicken breast):

- Calories: 250 kcal
- Carbohydrates: 2g
- Protein: 30g
- Fat: 13g
- Saturated Fat: 2.5g
- Fibre: 0g
- Sugar: 0g
- Sodium: 220mg

2. BAKED SALMON WITH DILL AND MUSTARD GLAZE

Servings: 4
Prep time: 10 minutes
Cooking time: 20 minutes

Ingredients:

- 4 salmon fillets (about 150g each)
- 2 tablespoons Dijon mustard
- 1 tablespoon olive oil
- 1 tablespoon fresh dill, chopped
- 1 teaspoon lemon juice
- 2 cloves garlic, minced
- Salt and pepper to taste
- Lemon wedges for serving (optional)
- Fresh dill sprigs for garnish (optional)

Directions:

1. Preheat the oven to 200°C (390°F). Line a baking sheet with parchment paper or lightly grease it with olive oil.
2. Mix the Dijon mustard, olive oil, chopped dill, lemon juice, minced garlic, salt, and pepper in a small bowl to make the glaze.
3. Place the salmon fillets on the prepared baking sheet.
4. Brush the glaze mixture over each salmon fillet, ensuring they are evenly coated.
5. Bake the salmon in the preheated oven for about 15-20 minutes, or until the fish is cooked through and flakes easily with a fork.
6. Remove the baking sheet from the oven and let the salmon rest for a few minutes before serving.
7. Garnish the Diabetic Baked Salmon with Dill and Mustard Glaze with fresh dill sprigs, and serve with lemon wedges, if desired.
8. Serve the baked salmon as a delectable and healthy main course.

Nutritional Information (per serving - 1 salmon fillet):

- Calories: 300 kcal
- Carbohydrates: 2g
- Protein: 30g
- Fat: 19g
- Saturated Fat: 3.5g
- Fibre: 0g
- Sugar: 0g
- Sodium: 240mg

3. TURKEY AND VEGETABLE STIR-FRY

Servings: 4
Prep time: 15 minutes
Cooking time: 15 minutes

Ingredients:

- 400g turkey breast, thinly sliced
- 2 tablespoons olive oil
- 1 red bell pepper, thinly sliced
- 1 yellow bell pepper, thinly sliced
- 1 medium carrot, julienned
- 100g broccoli florets
- 2 cloves garlic, minced
- 2 tablespoons low-sodium soy sauce
- 1 tablespoon oyster sauce
- 1 teaspoon sesame oil
- 1/2 teaspoon ground ginger
- Salt and pepper to taste
- Fresh coriander for garnish (optional)
- Steamed brown rice or cauliflower rice for serving (optional)

Directions:

1. Heat 1 tablespoon of olive oil over medium-high heat in a wok or large skillet.
2. Add the thinly sliced turkey breast to the wok and stir-fry until the turkey is cooked through and no longer pink. Remove the cooked turkey from the wok and set it aside.
3. In the same wok, add the remaining 1 tablespoon of olive oil.
4. Add the minced garlic, julienned carrot, and broccoli florets to the wok. Stir-fry for about 2-3 minutes until the vegetables are slightly tender.
5. Add the thinly sliced red and yellow bell peppers to the wok and stir-fry for another 2-3 minutes until all the vegetables are crisp-tender.
6. Return the cooked turkey to the wok with the vegetables.
7. Mix the low-sodium soy sauce, oyster sauce, sesame oil, ground ginger, salt, and pepper in a small bowl.
8. Pour the sauce mixture over the turkey and vegetables in the wok. Toss everything together until well coated and heated through.
9. Remove the wok from the heat.
10. Garnish the Diabetic Turkey and Vegetable Stir-Fry with fresh coriander, if desired.
11. Serve the stir-fry as a delicious and nutritious main course.

Nutritional Information (per serving - without rice):

- Calories: 250 kcal
- Carbohydrates: 8g
- Protein: 30g
- Fat: 11g
- Saturated Fat: 2g
- Fibre: 3g
- Sugar: 4g
- Sodium: 420mg

4. HERB-ROASTED PORK TENDERLOIN

Servings: 4
Prep time: 10 minutes
Cooking time: 25 minutes

Ingredients:

- 500g pork tenderloin
- 2 tablespoons olive oil
- 2 cloves garlic, minced
- 1 tablespoon fresh rosemary, chopped
- 1 tablespoon fresh thyme, chopped
- 1 tablespoon fresh parsley, chopped
- Zest of 1 lemon
- Salt and pepper to taste

Directions:

1. Preheat the oven to 200°C (390°F).
2. In a small bowl, mix the olive oil, minced garlic, chopped rosemary, chopped thyme, chopped parsley, lemon zest, salt, and pepper to make the herb rub.
3. Pat the pork tenderloin dry with paper towels.
4. Rub the herb mixture all over the pork tenderloin, ensuring it is evenly coated.
5. Place the seasoned pork tenderloin on a roasting pan or a baking sheet lined with parchment paper.
6. Roast the pork in the oven for about 20-25 minutes, or until it reaches an internal temperature of 70°C (160°F) and is cooked through.
7. Remove the pork tenderloin from the oven and let it rest for a few minutes before slicing.
8. Slice the Diabetic Herb-Roasted Pork Tenderloin and serve it as a delicious and protein-rich main course.

Nutritional Information (per serving):

- Calories: 250 kcal
- Carbohydrates: 1g
- Protein: 30g
- Fat: 14g
- Saturated Fat: 3g
- Fibre: 0g
- Sugar: 0g
- Sodium: 70mg

5. BEEF AND BROCCOLI SKEWERS

Servings: 4
Prep time: 20 minutes
Cooking time: 10 minutes

Ingredients:

- 400g beef sirloin or tenderloin, cut into 1-inch cubes
- 2 tablespoons low-sodium soy sauce
- 1 tablespoon olive oil
- 2 cloves garlic, minced
- 1 tablespoon fresh ginger, grated
- 2 tablespoons lemon juice
- 1 tablespoon brown sugar substitute (such as erythritol or stevia)
- 1 medium head of broccoli, cut into florets
- 1 red bell pepper, cut into chunks
- 1 red onion, cut into chunks
- Salt and pepper to taste
- Skewers (metal or wooden, soaked in water if using wooden skewers)

Directions:

1. Mix the low-sodium soy sauce, olive oil, minced garlic, grated ginger, lemon juice, and brown sugar substitute in a bowl to create the marinade.
2. Add the beef cubes to the marinade and toss them until evenly coated. Cover the bowl with cling film and refrigerate to marinate for at least 15 minutes.
3. Preheat the grill or grill pan to medium-high heat.
4. While the beef is marinating, blanch the broccoli florets in boiling water for about 2 minutes, then drain and rinse them under cold water to stop the cooking process.
5. Remove the beef from the marinade, reserving the marinade for basting.
6. Thread the marinated beef cubes, blanched broccoli florets, red bell pepper chunks, and red onion chunks alternately onto the skewers.
7. Season the skewers with salt and pepper to taste.
8. Grill the beef and broccoli skewers for about 3-5 minutes on each side, basting them with the reserved marinade occasionally until the beef is cooked to your desired level of doneness and the vegetables are tender-crisp.
9. Remove the skewers from the grill.
10. Serve the Diabetic Beef and Broccoli Skewers as a delightful and protein-rich main course.

Nutritional Information (per serving - 2 skewers):

- Calories: 250 kcal
- Carbohydrates: 8g
- Protein: 25g
- Fat: 12g
- Saturated Fat: 4g
- Fibre: 3g
- Sugar: 4g
- Sodium: 370mg

6. BAKED LEMON GARLIC SHRIMP

Servings: 4
Prep time: 15 minutes
Cooking time: 12 minutes

Ingredients:

- 500g large shrimp, peeled and deveined
- 3 tablespoons olive oil
- Zest of 1 lemon
- 2 tablespoons lemon juice
- 3 cloves garlic, minced
- 1 tablespoon fresh parsley, chopped
- Salt and pepper to taste
- Lemon wedges for serving (optional)
- Fresh parsley for garnish (optional)

Directions:

1. Preheat the oven to 200°C (390°F).
2. Mix the olive oil, lemon zest, lemon juice, minced garlic, chopped parsley, salt, and pepper in a bowl to create the marinade.
3. Add the peeled and deveined shrimp to the marinade and toss them until evenly coated. Let them marinate for about 10 minutes.
4. Line a baking sheet with parchment paper.
5. Arrange the marinated shrimp in a single layer on the prepared baking sheet.
6. Bake the shrimp in the preheated oven for about 10-12 minutes or until they are pink and opaque.
7. Remove the baking sheet from the oven.
8. Serve the Diabetic Baked Lemon Garlic Shrimp with lemon wedges and garnish with fresh parsley, if desired.
9. Serve the shrimp as a delectable, protein-rich main course or a delicious appetizer.

Nutritional Information (per serving):

- Calories: 180 kcal
- Carbohydrates: 1g
- Protein: 22g
- Fat: 9g
- Saturated Fat: 1g
- Fibre: 0g
- Sugar: 0g
- Sodium: 150mg

7. STUFFED BELL PEPPERS WITH GROUND TURKEY

Servings: 4

Prep time: 20 minutes

Cooking time: 40 minutes

Ingredients:

- 4 large bell peppers (any colour), tops removed and seeds discarded
- 400g lean ground turkey
- 1 tablespoon olive oil
- 1 small onion, finely chopped
- 2 cloves garlic, minced
- 1 teaspoon dried oregano
- 1 teaspoon dried basil
- 1/2 teaspoon ground cumin
- 400g canned chopped tomatoes (unsweetened)
- 50g grated mozzarella cheese (reduced-fat, optional)
- Salt and pepper to taste
- Fresh parsley for garnish (optional)

Directions:

1. Preheat the oven to 180°C (350°F).
2. In a large pan, heat the olive oil over medium heat. Add the chopped onion, minced garlic, and sauté until the onion becomes translucent.
3. Add the lean ground turkey to the pan, breaking it apart with a spoon, and cook until it is no longer pink and is fully cooked.
4. Stir in the dried oregano, dried basil, and ground cumin. Season with salt and pepper to taste.
5. Pour in the canned chopped tomatoes and let the mixture simmer for about 5 minutes.
6. While the turkey mixture is simmering, lightly steam the bell peppers by placing them in a microwave-safe dish with water, covering them with a microwave-safe lid, and microwaving them on high for 3-4 minutes until slightly softened.
7. Stuff each bell pepper with the cooked turkey mixture, pressing it down gently to fill the peppers.
8. Place the stuffed bell peppers in a baking dish, cover the dish with foil, and bake in the preheated oven for about 25 minutes.
9. If desired, remove the foil, sprinkle the grated mozzarella cheese over the tops of the stuffed peppers, and return the dish to the oven for another 5 minutes or until the cheese is melted and bubbly.
10. Remove the stuffed bell peppers from the oven.
11. Garnish the Diabetic Stuffed Bell Peppers with Ground Turkey with fresh parsley, if desired.
12. Serve the stuffed bell peppers as a wholesome and tasty main course.

Nutritional Information (per serving):

- Calories: 300 kcal
- Carbohydrates: 18g
- Protein: 28g
- Fat: 14g
- Saturated Fat: 3g
- Fibre: 5g
- Sugar: 9g
- Sodium: 320mg

8. HERB-CRUSTED BAKED CHICKEN THIGHS

Servings: 4
Prep time: 15 minutes
Cooking time: 25 minutes

Ingredients:

- 8 boneless, skinless chicken thighs
- 2 tablespoons olive oil
- 2 cloves garlic, minced
- 1 tablespoon fresh thyme, chopped
- 1 tablespoon fresh rosemary, chopped
- 1 tablespoon fresh parsley, chopped
- Zest of 1 lemon
- Salt and pepper to taste

Directions:

1. Preheat the oven to 200°C (390°F).
2. Mix the olive oil, minced garlic, chopped thyme, chopped rosemary, chopped parsley, lemon zest, salt, and pepper to create the herb crust.
3. Pat the chicken thighs dry with paper towels.
4. Dip each chicken thigh in the herb crust mixture, coating both sides evenly.
5. Place the herb-crusted chicken thighs on a baking sheet lined with parchment paper.
6. Bake the chicken in the preheated oven for about 20-25 minutes, or until they are cooked through, and the internal temperature reaches 75°C (165°F).
7. Remove the baking sheet from the oven.
8. Serve the Diabetic Herb-Crusted Baked Chicken Thighs as a delightful and protein-rich main course.

Nutritional Information (per serving - 2 chicken thighs):

- Calories: 300 kcal
- Carbohydrates: 0g
- Protein: 32g
- Fat: 18g
- Saturated Fat: 4g
- Fibre: 0g
- Sugar: 0g
- Sodium: 300mg

9. SPICY GRILLED FISH TACOS

Servings: 4
Prep time: 15 minutes
Cooking time: 10 minutes

Ingredients:

- 500g white fish fillets (such as cod or tilapia)
- 2 tablespoons olive oil
- 1 tablespoon lime juice
- 2 cloves garlic, minced
- 1 teaspoon ground cumin
- 1 teaspoon paprika
- 1/2 teaspoon cayenne pepper (adjust to your spice preference)
- Salt and pepper to taste
- 8 small whole-grain or low-carb tortillas
- 250g shredded lettuce
- 125g diced tomatoes
- 75g diced red onion
- Fresh coriander for garnish (optional)
- Lime wedges for serving (optional)

Directions:

1. Mix the olive oil, lime juice, minced garlic, ground cumin, paprika, cayenne pepper, salt, and pepper to create the marinade.
2. Pat the fish fillets dry with paper towels.
3. Dip each fish fillet in the marinade, coating both sides evenly.
4. Preheat the grill or grill pan to medium-high heat.
5. Grill the fish fillets on each side for 4-5 minutes until they are cooked through and flake easily with a fork.
6. While the fish grills warm the tortillas on the grill for about 1 minute on each side or until they are slightly toasted and pliable.
7. Remove the fish from the grill and let it rest for a few minutes before flaking it into smaller pieces with a fork.
8. Assemble the Diabetic Spicy Grilled Fish Tacos by placing some shredded lettuce on each tortilla, followed by the flaked fish.
9. Top the tacos with diced tomatoes and red onion.
10. Garnish the tacos with fresh coriander, if desired.
11. Serve the Spicy Grilled Fish Tacos as a delectable and low-carb main course.

Nutritional Information (per serving - 2 tacos):

- Calories: 300 kcal
- Carbohydrates: 20g
- Protein: 25g
- Fat: 12g
- Saturated Fat: 2g
- Fibre: 5g
- Sugar: 2g
- Sodium: 250mg

10. BALSAMIC-GLAZED PORK CHOPS

Servings: 4
Prep time: 10 minutes
Cooking time: 15 minutes

Ingredients:

- 4 boneless pork chops (about 150g each)
- 2 tablespoons olive oil
- 3 tablespoons balsamic vinegar
- 2 tablespoons low-sodium soy sauce
- 1 tablespoon Dijon mustard
- 2 cloves garlic, minced
- 1 tablespoon fresh rosemary, chopped
- Salt and pepper to taste

Directions:

1. Mix the olive oil, balsamic vinegar, low-sodium soy sauce, Dijon mustard, minced garlic, chopped rosemary, salt, and pepper to create the glaze.
2. Pat the pork chops dry with paper towels.
3. Dip each pork chop in the balsamic glaze, coating both sides evenly.
4. Preheat a non-stick pan over medium-high heat.
5. Add the pork chops to the pan and cook for about 5-7 minutes on each side until they reach an internal temperature of 70°C (160°F) and are cooked through.
6. While cooking the pork chops, you can baste them with the remaining glaze in the bowl to enhance the flavour.
7. Remove the pork chops from the pan and let them rest for a few minutes before serving.
8. Serve the Diabetic Balsamic-Glazed Pork Chops as a delightful and protein-rich main course.

Nutritional Information (per serving):

- Calories: 250 kcal
- Carbohydrates: 4g
- Protein: 25g
- Fat: 14g
- Saturated Fat: 3g
- Fibre: 0g
- Sugar: 2g
- Sodium: 300mg

11. LEMON GARLIC HERB SHRIMP SKEWERS

Servings: 4
Prep time: 20 minutes
Cooking time: 5 minutes

Ingredients:

- 500g large shrimp, peeled and deveined
- 2 tablespoons olive oil
- Zest of 1 lemon
- Juice of 1 lemon
- 3 cloves garlic, minced
- 1 tablespoon fresh parsley, chopped
- 1 tablespoon fresh thyme, chopped
- 1 tablespoon fresh rosemary, chopped
- Salt and pepper to taste
- Skewers (metal or wooden, soaked in water if using wooden skewers)

Directions:

1. Mix the olive oil, lemon zest, lemon juice, minced garlic, chopped parsley, chopped thyme, chopped rosemary, salt, and pepper to create the marinade.
2. Pat the shrimp dry with paper towels.
3. Dip each shrimp in the marinade, coating them evenly.
4. Cover the bowl with cling film and refrigerate for 10 minutes to marinate.
5. Preheat the grill or grill pan to medium-high heat.
6. Thread the marinated shrimp onto the skewers.
7. Grill the shrimp skewers on each side for about 2-3 minutes until they are pink and opaque.
8. Remove the shrimp skewers from the grill.
9. Serve the Diabetic Lemon Garlic Herb Shrimp Skewers as a delectable, protein-rich main course or appetizer.

Nutritional Information (per serving - 2 skewers):

- Calories: 180 kcal
- Carbohydrates: 2g
- Protein: 25g
- Fat: 8g
- Saturated Fat: 1g
- Fibre: 0g
- Sugar: 0g
- Sodium: 300mg

12. BAKED GREEK CHICKEN DRUMSTICKS

Servings: 4
Prep time: 10 minutes
Cooking time: 35 minutes

Ingredients:

- 8 chicken drumsticks
- 2 tablespoons olive oil
- Juice of 1 lemon
- 2 cloves garlic, minced
- 1 teaspoon dried oregano
- 1 teaspoon dried thyme
- 1 teaspoon dried rosemary
- 1/2 teaspoon dried basil
- Salt and pepper to taste
- Lemon wedges and fresh parsley for serving (optional)

Directions:

1. Mix the olive oil, lemon juice, minced garlic, dried oregano, dried thyme, rosemary, basil, salt, and pepper to create the marinade.
2. Pat the chicken drumsticks dry with paper towels.
3. Dip each drumstick in the marinade, coating them evenly.
4. Cover the bowl with cling film and refrigerate for at least 30 minutes to marinate.
5. Preheat the oven to 200°C (390°F).
6. Line a baking sheet with parchment paper.
7. Place the marinated chicken drumsticks on the prepared baking sheet.
8. Bake the chicken in the preheated oven for about 30-35 minutes, or until it reaches an internal temperature of 75°C (165°F) and is cooked through.
9. Remove the baking sheet from the oven.
10. Serve the Diabetic Baked Greek Chicken Drumsticks as a delicious and protein-rich main course.

Nutritional Information (per serving - 2 drumsticks):

- Calories: 350 kcal
- Carbohydrates: 2g
- Protein: 30g
- Fat: 24g
- Saturated Fat: 5g
- Fibre: 0g
- Sugar: 1g
- Sodium: 250mg

13. TURKEY CHILI

Servings: 6
Prep time: 15 minutes
Cooking time: 40 minutes

Ingredients:

- 500g lean ground turkey
- 1 tablespoon olive oil
- 1 large onion, chopped
- 2 cloves garlic, minced
- 1 red bell pepper, chopped
- 1 yellow bell pepper, chopped
- 2 medium carrots, diced
- 1 can (400g) chopped tomatoes (unsweetened)
- 1 can (400g) red kidney beans, drained and rinsed
- 1 tablespoon chilli powder
- 1 teaspoon ground cumin
- 1 teaspoon dried oregano
- 1/2 teaspoon smoked paprika
- 1/4 teaspoon cayenne pepper (adjust to your spice preference)
- Salt and pepper to taste
- 500ml low-sodium chicken or vegetable broth
- Fresh parsley or coriander for garnish (optional)

Directions:

1. In a large pot, heat the olive oil over medium heat. Add the chopped onion, minced garlic, and sauté until the onion becomes translucent.
2. Add the lean ground turkey to the pot and cook until it is no longer pink and is fully cooked.
3. Stir in the chopped red and yellow bell peppers, diced carrots, chopped tomatoes, and drained red kidney beans.
4. Season the mixture with chilli powder, ground cumin, dried oregano, smoked paprika, cayenne pepper, salt, and pepper. Stir everything together to combine the flavours.
5. Pour in the low-sodium chicken or vegetable broth and bring the mixture to a boil.
6. Reduce the heat to low, cover the pot with a lid, and let the chilli simmer for about 30 minutes, allowing the flavours to meld together.
7. After 30 minutes, check the seasoning and adjust the salt and pepper to taste.
8. Serve the Diabetic Turkey Chili hot, garnished with fresh parsley or coriander, if desired.

Nutritional Information (per serving):

- Calories: 250 kcal
- Carbohydrates: 20g
- Protein: 25g
- Fat: 8g
- Saturated Fat: 2g
- Fibre: 6g
- Sugar: 6g
- Sodium: 400mg

14. BEEF AND CABBAGE SKILLET

Servings: 4
Prep time: 10 minutes
Cooking time: 25 minutes

Ingredients:

- 500g lean ground beef
- 1 tablespoon olive oil
- 1 large onion, chopped
- 2 cloves garlic, minced
- 1 small head of cabbage, thinly sliced
- 2 medium carrots, grated
- 1 can (400g) chopped tomatoes (unsweetened)
- 2 tablespoons tomato paste
- 1 teaspoon dried thyme
- 1 teaspoon dried oregano
- 1/2 teaspoon paprika
- Salt and pepper to taste
- Fresh parsley for garnish (optional)

Directions:

1. In a large skillet, heat the olive oil over medium heat. Add the chopped onion, minced garlic, and sauté until the onion becomes translucent.
2. Add the lean ground beef to the skillet until it is browned and cooked.
3. Stir in the thinly sliced cabbage and grated carrots, and cook for a few minutes until the vegetables soften.
4. Pour the chopped tomatoes and tomato paste, and combine all the ingredients.
5. Season the mixture with dried thyme, dried oregano, paprika, salt, and pepper. Stir everything together to distribute the flavours.
6. Cover the skillet with a lid and let the mixture simmer on low heat for about 15 minutes, allowing the flavours to meld together and the vegetables to become tender.
7. After 15 minutes, check the seasoning and adjust the salt and pepper to taste.
8. Serve the Beef and Cabbage Skillet hot, garnished with fresh parsley, if desired.

Nutritional Information (per serving):

- Calories: 300 kcal
- Carbohydrates: 15g
- Protein: 25g
- Fat: 15g
- Saturated Fat: 5g
- Fibre: 6g
- Sugar: 9g
- Sodium: 400mg

15. LEMON HERB BAKED FISH WITH VEGETABLES

Servings: 4
Prep time: 15 minutes
Cooking time: 20 minutes

Ingredients:

- 4 white fish fillets (such as cod or haddock), about 150g each
- 2 tablespoons olive oil
- Zest of 1 lemon
- Juice of 1 lemon
- 2 cloves garlic, minced
- 1 tablespoon fresh parsley, chopped
- 1 tablespoon fresh thyme, chopped
- 1 tablespoon fresh rosemary, chopped
- 1/2 teaspoon dried oregano
- Salt and pepper to taste
- 2 medium zucchinis, sliced
- 1 red bell pepper, sliced
- 1 yellow bell pepper, sliced
- 1 small red onion, sliced

Directions:

1. Preheat the oven to 200°C (390°F).
2. Mix the olive oil, lemon zest, lemon juice, minced garlic, chopped parsley, chopped thyme, chopped rosemary, dried oregano, salt, and pepper to create the marinade.
3. Pat the fish fillets dry with paper towels.
4. Dip each fish fillet in the marinade, coating both sides evenly.
5. Toss the sliced zucchini, red bell pepper, yellow bell pepper, and red onion with olive oil, salt, and pepper in a separate bowl.
6. Place the marinated fish fillets and the seasoned vegetables on a baking sheet lined with parchment paper.
7. Bake in the preheated oven for about 15-20 minutes, or until the fish is cooked through and flakes easily with a fork, and the vegetables are tender and slightly caramelized.
8. Remove the baking sheet from the oven.
9. Serve the Diabetic Lemon Herb Baked Fish with Vegetables hot, garnished with additional fresh herbs if desired.

Nutritional Information (per serving):

- Calories: 250 kcal
- Carbohydrates: 10g
- Protein: 25g
- Fat: 12g
- Saturated Fat: 2g
- Fibre: 3g
- Sugar: 5g
- Sodium: 200mg

16. MEDITERRANEAN CHICKEN AND QUINOA

Servings: 4
Prep time: 15 minutes
Cooking time: 25 minutes

Ingredients:

- 4 boneless, skinless chicken breasts
- 2 tablespoons olive oil
- 2 cloves garlic, minced
- 1 teaspoon dried oregano
- 1 teaspoon dried thyme
- 1 teaspoon dried rosemary
- Zest of 1 lemon
- Juice of 1 lemon
- Salt and pepper to taste
- 200g quinoa
- 400ml low-sodium chicken or vegetable broth
- 1 red bell pepper, diced
- 1 yellow bell pepper, diced
- 1 small cucumber, diced
- 200g cherry tomatoes, halved
- 50g pitted Kalamata olives, chopped
- 2 tablespoons chopped fresh parsley
- 2 tablespoons chopped fresh mint
- 50g crumbled feta cheese (optional)

Directions:

1. Mix the olive oil, minced garlic, dried oregano, dried thyme, rosemary, lemon zest, lemon juice, salt, and pepper to create the marinade.
2. Pat the chicken breasts dry with paper towels.
3. Dip each chicken breast in the marinade, coating both sides evenly.
4. Cover the bowl with cling film and refrigerate for 30 minutes to marinate.
5. In a saucepan, rinse the quinoa thoroughly under cold water. Drain and add the quinoa to the saucepan and the low-sodium chicken or vegetable broth.
6. Bring the quinoa to a boil over medium heat. Reduce the heat to low, cover the saucepan with a lid, and let it simmer for about 15 minutes or until the quinoa is cooked and the liquid is absorbed.
7. In the meantime, preheat a non-stick pan over medium-high heat.
8. Add the marinated chicken breasts to the pan and cook for 4-5 minutes on each side until they are cooked through and no longer pink in the centre.
9. Remove the chicken breasts from the pan and let them rest for a few minutes before slicing.
10. Combine the diced red and yellow bell peppers, cucumber, halved cherry tomatoes, chopped olives, chopped parsley, and chopped mint in a large mixing bowl.
11. Add the cooked quinoa to the bowl and toss everything together to mix well.
12. Serve the Diabetic Mediterranean Chicken and Quinoa with the sliced chicken breasts on top.
13. If desired, sprinkle some crumbled feta cheese over the dish for added flavour.

Nutritional Information (per serving):

- Calories: 450 kcal
- Carbohydrates: 40g
- Protein: 35g
- Fat: 18g
- Saturated Fat: 4g
- Fibre: 6g
- Sugar: 5g
- Sodium: 400mg

17. SAUSAGE AND VEGETABLE SHEET PAN DINNER

Servings: 4
Prep time: 15 minutes
Cooking time: 25 minutes

Ingredients:

- 8 pork or chicken sausages (choose low-sodium and lean options)
- 2 tablespoons olive oil
- 1 teaspoon dried oregano
- 1 teaspoon dried thyme
- 1 teaspoon dried rosemary
- 1/2 teaspoon paprika
- Salt and pepper to taste
- 500g baby potatoes, halved
- 2 medium carrots, peeled and cut into chunks
- 1 red bell pepper, sliced
- 1 yellow bell pepper, sliced
- 1 small red onion, sliced
- 2 cloves garlic, minced
- Fresh parsley for garnish (optional)

Directions:

1. Preheat the oven to 200°C (390°F).
2. Mix the olive oil, dried oregano, dried thyme, rosemary, paprika, salt, and pepper in a bowl to create the seasoning.
3. Add the halved baby potatoes, carrot chunks, sliced red and yellow bell peppers, sliced red onion, and minced garlic to the bowl with the seasoning. Toss everything together to coat the vegetables evenly with the seasoning.
4. Line a large baking sheet with parchment paper.
5. Arrange the sausages and seasoned vegetables on the baking sheet in a single layer.
6. Roast in the oven for about 20-25 minutes, or until the sausages are cooked and the vegetables are tender and slightly caramelized.
7. Remove the baking sheet from the oven.
8. Serve the Diabetic Sausage and Vegetable Sheet Pan Dinner hot, garnished with fresh parsley if desired.

Nutritional Information (per serving):

- Calories: 400 kcal
- Carbohydrates: 25g
- Protein: 20g
- Fat: 25g
- Saturated Fat: 6g
- Fibre: 5g
- Sugar: 5g
- Sodium: 450mg

18. ITALIAN-STYLE BEEF AND CABBAGE STEW

Servings: 6
Prep time: 15 minutes
Cooking time: 1 hour 30 minutes

Ingredients:

- 500g lean beef stew meat, cubed
- 2 tablespoons olive oil
- 1 large onion, chopped
- 2 cloves garlic, minced
- 2 carrots, peeled and diced
- 2 celery stalks, diced
- 1 small head of cabbage, shredded
- 1 can (400g) chopped tomatoes (unsweetened)
- 500ml low-sodium beef broth
- 1 teaspoon dried basil
- 1 teaspoon dried oregano
- 1/2 teaspoon dried thyme
- Salt and pepper to taste
- Fresh parsley for garnish (optional)

Directions:

1. Heat the olive oil over medium heat in a large pot or Dutch oven. Add the chopped onion, minced garlic, and sauté until the onion becomes translucent.
2. Add the cubed lean beef stew meat to the pot and cook until it is browned on all sides.
3. Stir in the diced carrots and celery, and cook for a few minutes until they soften.
4. Add the shredded cabbage to the pot and stir with the other ingredients.
5. Pour in the chopped tomatoes and low-sodium beef broth, and add the dried basil, dried oregano, dried thyme, salt, and pepper. Stir everything together to mix the flavours.
6. Bring the stew to a boil over medium-high heat, then reduce the heat to low. Cover the pot with a lid and let the stew simmer for about 1 hour or until the beef is tender and the flavours have melded together.
7. After 1 hour, check the seasoning and adjust the salt and pepper to taste.
8. Serve the Diabetic Italian-Style Beef and Cabbage Stew hot, garnished with fresh parsley if desired.

Nutritional Information (per serving):

- Calories: 250 kcal
- Carbohydrates: 15g
- Protein: 20g
- Fat: 10g
- Saturated Fat: 3g
- Fibre: 6g
- Sugar: 8g
- Sodium: 350mg

19. COCONUT CURRY CHICKEN WITH CAULIFLOWER RICE

Servings: 4
Prep time: 15 minutes
Cooking time: 25 minutes

Ingredients: For the Coconut Curry Chicken:

- 500g boneless, skinless chicken breasts cut into bite-sized pieces
- 2 tablespoons olive oil
- 1 large onion, chopped
- 2 cloves garlic, minced
- 1 tablespoon grated ginger
- 1 red bell pepper, sliced
- 1 yellow bell pepper, sliced
- 1 can (400g) coconut milk (unsweetened)
- 2 tablespoons red curry paste (check for low-sugar options)
- 1 tablespoon low-sodium soy sauce
- 1 teaspoon ground turmeric
- 1 teaspoon ground cumin
- Salt and pepper to taste
- Fresh coriander for garnish (optional)

For the Cauliflower Rice:

- 1 medium head of cauliflower, grated or finely chopped
- 1 tablespoon olive oil
- Salt and pepper to taste

Directions:

1. Heat the olive oil over medium heat in a large skillet or wok. Add the chopped onion, minced garlic, and grated ginger, and sauté until the onion becomes translucent.
2. Add the bite-sized chicken pieces to the skillet and cook until they are browned and cooked through.
3. Stir in the sliced red and yellow bell peppers, and cook for a few minutes until they soften.
4. Whisk together the coconut milk, red curry paste, low-sodium soy sauce, ground turmeric, ground cumin, salt, and pepper in a bowl.
5. Pour the coconut milk mixture into the skillet with the chicken and vegetables. Stir everything together to coat the chicken and vegetables with the curry sauce.
6. Cover the skillet with a lid and let the curry simmer for 10-15 minutes, allowing the flavours to meld together.
7. While the curry is simmering, make the cauliflower rice. Grate or finely chop the cauliflower into rice-like pieces.
8. In a separate pan, heat the olive oil over medium heat. Add the cauliflower rice and sauté for a few minutes until it becomes tender—season with salt and pepper to taste.
9. Serve the Diabetic Coconut Curry Chicken over the cauliflower rice, and garnish with fresh coriander if desired.

Nutritional Information (per serving):

- Calories: 400 kcal
- Carbohydrates: 15g
- Protein: 25g
- Fat: 25g
- Saturated Fat: 12g
- Fibre: 5g
- Sugar: 6g
- Sodium: 450mg

20. BEEF AND BROCCOLI QUINOA SKILLET

Servings: 4
Prep time: 15 minutes
Cooking time: 25 minutes

Ingredients:

- 500g lean beef steak, thinly sliced
- 2 tablespoons olive oil
- 2 cloves garlic, minced
- 1 teaspoon grated ginger
- 2 tablespoons low-sodium soy sauce
- 2 tablespoons oyster sauce (check for low-sugar options)
- 1 tablespoon sesame oil
- 1 head of broccoli, cut into florets
- 500g mushrooms
- 1 red bell pepper, sliced
- 1 yellow bell pepper, sliced
- 200g cooked quinoa
- Sesame seeds for garnish (optional)
- Fresh coriander for garnish (optional)

Directions:

1. Heat 1 tablespoon of olive oil over medium heat in a large skillet or wok. Add the thinly sliced beef and cook until it is browned and cooked to your desired level of doneness. Remove the meat from the skillet and set it aside.
2. In the same skillet, add the remaining 1 tablespoon of olive oil. Sauté the minced garlic and grated ginger until they become fragrant.
3. Add the broccoli florets, mushrooms, sliced red and yellow bell peppers to the skillet and stir-fry for a few minutes until the vegetables soften.
4. Mix the low-sodium soy sauce, oyster sauce, and sesame oil in a small bowl. Pour the sauce mixture over the vegetables in the skillet and stir to coat them evenly.
5. Add the cooked quinoa to the skillet and stir-fry with the vegetables and sauce until everything is well combined.
6. Return the cooked beef to the skillet, and toss everything together until the beef is heated through.
7. Serve the Diabetic Beef and Broccoli Quinoa Skillet hot, garnished with sesame seeds and fresh coriander if desired.

Nutritional Information (per serving):

- Calories: 400 kcal
- Carbohydrates: 25g
- Protein: 30g
- Fat: 20g
- Saturated Fat: 4g
- Fibre: 6g
- Sugar: 5g
- Sodium: 400mg

21. LEMON GARLIC SHRIMP AND SPINACH ORZO

Servings: 4
Prep time: 10 minutes
Cooking time: 15 minutes

Ingredients:

- 300g large shrimp, peeled and deveined
- 250g whole wheat orzo pasta
- 2 tablespoons olive oil
- 4 cloves garlic, minced
- Zest of 1 lemon
- Juice of 1 lemon
- 150g baby spinach leaves
- 2 tablespoons chopped fresh parsley
- Salt and pepper to taste
- Grated Parmesan cheese for garnish (optional)

Directions:

1. Cook the whole wheat orzo pasta according to the package instructions until al dente. Drain the cooked orzo and set it aside.
2. In a large skillet, heat the olive oil over medium heat. Add the minced garlic and sauté for about 1 minute until it becomes fragrant.
3. Add the peeled and deveined shrimp to the skillet, and cook them for 2-3 minutes on each side until they turn pink and are cooked through.
4. Add the cooked orzo pasta to the skillet with the shrimp, and toss everything together to combine.
5. Stir in the lemon zest and lemon juice, coating the shrimp and orzo with the refreshing lemon flavour.
6. Add the baby spinach leaves to the skillet and toss everything together until the spinach wilts slightly.
7. Season the Lemon Garlic Shrimp and Spinach Orzo with salt and pepper to taste.
8. Sprinkle chopped fresh parsley over the dish, and if desired, garnish with grated Parmesan cheese for added flavour.
9. Serve the Diabetic Lemon Garlic Shrimp and Spinach Orzo hot and enjoy!

Nutritional Information (per serving):

- Calories: 350 kcal
- Carbohydrates: 40g
- Protein: 20g
- Fat: 12g
- Saturated Fat: 2g
- Fibre: 5g
- Sugar: 2g
- Sodium: 300mg

22. MEXICAN CAULIFLOWER RICE WITH CHICKEN

Servings: 4
Prep time: 15 minutes
Cooking time: 25 minutes

Ingredients:

- 500g boneless, skinless chicken breasts cut into bite-sized pieces
- 1 tablespoon olive oil
- 1 small onion, chopped
- 2 cloves garlic, minced
- 1 red bell pepper, diced
- 1 green bell pepper, diced
- 1 can (400g) chopped tomatoes (unsweetened)
- 1 tablespoon tomato paste
- 1 tablespoon ground cumin
- 1 tablespoon chilli powder
- 1 teaspoon paprika
- 1 teaspoon dried oregano
- Salt and pepper to taste
- 1 medium head of cauliflower, grated or finely chopped
- Fresh coriander for garnish (optional)
- Lime wedges for serving (optional)

Directions:

1. Heat the olive oil over medium heat in a large skillet or frying pan. Add the chopped onion, minced garlic, and sauté until the onion becomes translucent.
2. Add the bite-sized chicken pieces to the skillet and cook until they are browned and cooked through.
3. Stir in the diced red and green bell peppers, and cook for a few minutes until they soften.
4. Add the chopped tomatoes and tomato paste to the skillet, and stir everything together.
5. Season the mixture with ground cumin, chilli powder, paprika, dried oregano, salt, and pepper. Stir to ensure the spices are evenly distributed.
6. Add the grated or finely chopped cauliflower to the skillet, and mix it in with the chicken and vegetable mixture.
7. Cover the skillet with a lid and cook for about 8-10 minutes or until the cauliflower is tender.
8. Serve the Diabetic Mexican Cauliflower Rice with hot chicken, garnished with fresh coriander and lime wedges if desired.

Nutritional Information (per serving):

- Calories: 300 kcal
- Carbohydrates: 15g
- Protein: 25g
- Fat: 10g
- Saturated Fat: 2g
- Fibre: 5g
- Sugar: 8g
- Sodium: 450mg

23. MOROCCAN LAMB AND VEGETABLE TAGINE

Servings: 4
Prep time: 20 minutes
Cooking time: 1 hour 30 minutes

Ingredients:

- 500g lean lamb stew meat, cubed
- 2 tablespoons olive oil
- 1 large onion, chopped
- 2 cloves garlic, minced
- 1 teaspoon ground cumin
- 1 teaspoon ground coriander
- 1 teaspoon ground cinnamon
- 1/2 teaspoon ground ginger
- 1/2 teaspoon ground paprika
- 1/4 teaspoon ground turmeric
- Salt and pepper to taste
- 2 carrots, peeled and cut into chunks
- 2 parsnips, peeled and cut into chunks
- 1 large sweet potato, peeled and cut into chunks
- 1 can (400g) chopped tomatoes (unsweetened)
- 500ml low-sodium vegetable or chicken broth
- 2 tablespoons chopped fresh coriander
- Fresh coriander leaves for garnish (optional)
- Lemon wedges for serving (optional)

Directions:

1. Heat the olive oil over medium heat in a large tagine or a heavy-bottomed pot. Add the chopped onion, minced garlic, and sauté until the onion becomes translucent.
2. Add the cubed lean lamb stew meat to the tagine, and cook until it is browned on all sides.
3. Stir in the ground cumin, coriander, cinnamon, ginger, paprika, turmeric, salt, and pepper. Coat the lamb with aromatic spices.
4. Add the chopped carrots, parsnips, and sweet potato to the tagine, and mix everything.
5. Pour in the chopped tomatoes and low-sodium vegetable or chicken broth, and stir to combine all the ingredients.
6. Cover the tagine with a lid and let it simmer on low heat for about 1 hour or until the lamb and vegetables become tender.
7. Stir in the chopped fresh coriander just before serving.
8. Serve the Diabetic Moroccan Lamb and Vegetable Tagine hot, garnished with fresh coriander leaves and lemon wedges if desired.

Nutritional Information (per serving):

- Calories: 400 kcal
- Carbohydrates: 25g
- Protein: 30g
- Fat: 15g
- Saturated Fat: 3g
- Fibre: 6g
- Sugar: 10g
- Sodium: 400mg

CHAPTER 5

VEGITARIAN MAIN COURSES

1. GRILLED PORTOBELLO MUSHROOM STEAKS

Servings: 4
Prep time: 15 minutes
Cooking time: 10 minutes

Ingredients:

- 4 large portobello mushrooms
- 2 tablespoons olive oil
- 2 cloves garlic, minced
- 1 tablespoon balsamic vinegar
- 1 tablespoon low-sodium soy sauce
- 1 teaspoon dried thyme
- 1 teaspoon dried rosemary
- Salt and pepper to taste
- Fresh parsley for garnish (optional)

Directions:

1. Clean the portobello mushrooms using a damp cloth or paper towel to remove any dirt. Remove the stems if they are tough, and discard them.
2. Whisk together the olive oil, minced garlic, balsamic vinegar, low-sodium soy sauce, dried thyme, rosemary, salt, and pepper in a shallow dish to create the marinade.
3. Place the cleaned portobello mushrooms in the marinade, turning them to coat both sides. Let them marinate for at least 10 minutes, allowing the flavours to infuse.
4. Preheat the grill to medium-high heat.
5. Remove the marinated mushrooms from the dish, shaking off any excess marinade, and place them directly on the grill.
6. Grill the portobello mushrooms on each side for 4-5 minutes until they become tender and grill marks appear.
7. While grilling, baste the mushrooms with the remaining marinade to enhance the flavour.
8. Once cooked, remove the grilled portobello mushroom steaks from the grill and let them rest for a minute.
9. Serve the Diabetic Grilled Portobello Mushroom Steaks hot, garnished with fresh parsley if desired.

Nutritional Information (per serving):

- Calories: 100 kcal
- Carbohydrates: 5g
- Protein: 3g
- Fat: 7g
- Saturated Fat: 1g
- Fibre: 2g
- Sugar: 2g
- Sodium: 200mg

2. LENTIL AND VEGETABLE STIR-FRY

Servings: 4
Prep time: 10 minutes
Cooking time: 25 minutes

Ingredients:

- 200g dried green lentils
- 2 tablespoons olive oil
- 1 large onion, thinly sliced
- 2 cloves garlic, minced
- 1 red bell pepper, thinly sliced
- 1 yellow bell pepper, thinly sliced
- 1 small courgette (zucchini), thinly sliced
- 100g baby corn, halved
- 100g sugar snap peas
- 2 tablespoons low-sodium soy sauce
- 1 tablespoon rice vinegar
- 1 tablespoon toasted sesame oil
- 1 teaspoon grated ginger
- 1 teaspoon chilli flakes (optional)
- Salt and pepper to taste
- Fresh coriander for garnish (optional)

Directions:

1. Rinse the dried green lentils thoroughly in cold water. Cook the lentils according to the package instructions until they are tender but not mushy. Drain any excess water and set the lentils aside.
2. Heat the olive oil over medium-high heat in a large wok or frying pan. Add the thinly sliced onion and sauté until it becomes soft and translucent.
3. Add the minced garlic to the pan and cook for another minute until it becomes fragrant.
4. Stir in the sliced red and yellow bell peppers, courgette, baby corn, and sugar snap peas. Cook for a few minutes until the vegetables soften but remain crisp.
5. Add the cooked green lentils to the pan with the vegetables, and toss everything together.
6. In a small bowl, whisk together the low-sodium soy sauce, rice vinegar, toasted sesame oil, grated ginger, and chilli flakes (if using).
7. Pour the sauce over the lentil and vegetable mixture into the pan. Stir everything together to coat the vegetables and lentils with the delicious sauce.
8. Season the Lentil and Vegetable Stir-Fry with salt and pepper to taste.
9. Serve the Diabetic Lentil and Vegetable Stir-Fry hot, garnished with fresh coriander if desired.

Nutritional Information (per serving):

- Calories: 250 kcal
- Carbohydrates: 35g
- Protein: 12g
- Fat: 8g
- Saturated Fat: 1g
- Fibre: 12g
- Sugar: 7g
- Sodium: 350mg

3. EGGPLANT PARMESAN

Servings: 4
Prep time: 30 minutes
Cooking time: 40 minutes

Ingredients:

- 1 large eggplant, sliced into 1/4-inch rounds
- 2 large eggs
- 100g almond flour (ground almonds)
- 50g grated Parmesan cheese
- 1 teaspoon dried oregano
- 1 teaspoon dried basil
- 1/2 teaspoon garlic powder
- 1/4 teaspoon salt
- 1/4 teaspoon black pepper
- 500ml sugar-free tomato sauce
- 200g shredded mozzarella cheese
- Olive oil for frying
- Fresh basil leaves for garnish (optional)

Directions:

1. Preheat the oven to 190°C (375°F).
2. In a shallow dish, whisk the eggs until well beaten.
3. Mix the almond flour, grated Parmesan cheese, dried oregano, dried basil, garlic powder, salt, and black pepper in another shallow dish.
4. Dip each eggplant round into the beaten eggs, ensuring both sides are coated.
5. Dredge the egg-coated eggplant rounds in the almond flour mixture, pressing gently to adhere the mixture to the eggplant.
6. Heat enough olive oil to cover the bottom of the pan in a large frying pan. Fry the coated eggplant rounds in batches until they are golden brown on both sides. Place the cooked eggplant rounds on a paper towel-lined plate to remove excess oil.
7. In a baking dish, spread a thin layer of sugar-free tomato sauce on the bottom.
8. Arrange half the fried eggplant rounds in a single layer over the tomato sauce.
9. Sprinkle half of the shredded mozzarella cheese over the eggplant.
10. Repeat the layers with the remaining eggplant rounds and mozzarella cheese.
11. Top the Eggplant Parmesan with a final layer of sugar-free tomato sauce.
12. Bake the Eggplant Parmesan in the oven for about 25 minutes or until the cheese is melted and bubbly.
13. Let the dish rest for a few minutes before serving.
14. Serve the Diabetic Eggplant Parmesan hot, garnished with fresh basil leaves if desired.

Nutritional Information (per serving):

- Calories: 300 kcal
- Carbohydrates: 15g
- Protein: 18g
- Fat: 20g
- Saturated Fat: 6g
- Fibre: 6g
- Sugar: 5g
- Sodium: 600mg

4. CAULIFLOWER FRIED RICE

Servings: 4
Prep time: 15 minutes
Cooking time: 15 minutes

Ingredients:

- 1 medium head of cauliflower
- 2 tablespoons olive oil
- 1 small onion, finely chopped
- 2 cloves garlic, minced
- 1 small carrot, diced
- 100g frozen peas
- 2 tablespoons low-sodium soy sauce
- 1 tablespoon rice vinegar
- 2 large eggs, beaten
- Salt and pepper to taste
- Fresh spring onions for garnish (optional)

Directions:

1. Wash the cauliflower and remove the leaves and stem. Cut the cauliflower into florets and place them in a food processor. Pulse until the cauliflower resembles rice-like grains. Alternatively, you can use a grater to achieve a similar texture. Set the cauliflower rice aside.
2. Heat the olive oil over medium heat in a large frying pan or wok. Add the finely chopped onion and sauté until it becomes soft and translucent.
3. Add the minced garlic to the pan and cook for another minute until it becomes fragrant.
4. Stir in the diced carrot and frozen peas. Cook for a few minutes until the vegetables start to soften.
5. Push the vegetables to one side of the pan and add the beaten eggs to the other side. Scramble the eggs until they are fully cooked.
6. Mix the cooked eggs with the vegetables in the pan.
7. Add the cauliflower rice to the pan and toss everything together.
8. Whisk together the low-sodium soy sauce and rice vinegar in a small bowl.
9. Pour the sauce over the cauliflower rice and stir to coat everything with the delicious flavours.
10. Season the Diabetic Cauliflower Fried Rice with salt and pepper to taste.
11. Cook for 2-3 minutes, stirring occasionally, until the cauliflower rice is heated through.
12. Serve the Diabetic Cauliflower Fried Rice hot, garnished with fresh spring onions if desired.

Nutritional Information (per serving):

- Calories: 150 kcal
- Carbohydrates: 10g
- Protein: 7g
- Fat: 8g
- Saturated Fat: 1g
- Fibre: 5g
- Sugar: 5g
- Sodium: 250mg

5. SPINACH AND FETA STUFFED PEPPERS

Servings: 4
Prep time: 20 minutes
Cooking time: 30 minutes

Ingredients:

- 4 large bell peppers (any colour), halved and seeds removed
- 200g frozen chopped spinach, thawed and excess water squeezed out
- 100g crumbled feta cheese
- 1 small onion, finely chopped
- 2 cloves garlic, minced
- 1 tablespoon olive oil
- 1 teaspoon dried oregano
- 1 teaspoon dried basil
- 1/2 teaspoon dried thyme
- Salt and pepper to taste
- 1 tablespoon grated Parmesan cheese (optional)
- Fresh parsley for garnish (optional)

Directions:

1. Preheat the oven to 200°C (400°F).
2. In a large frying pan, heat the olive oil over medium heat. Add the finely chopped onion and sauté until it becomes soft and translucent.
3. Add the minced garlic to the pan and cook for another minute until it becomes fragrant.
4. Stir in the thawed chopped spinach, dried oregano, dried basil, dried thyme, salt, and pepper. Cook for a few minutes until the spinach is heated and the flavours are well combined.
5. Remove the pan from heat and let the mixture cool slightly.
6. Mix the cooked spinach mixture in a bowl with the crumbled feta cheese.
7. Stuff each halved bell pepper with the spinach and feta mixture.
8. Place the stuffed peppers on a baking tray or dish.
9. Optionally, sprinkle the grated Parmesan cheese on top of the stuffed peppers for an extra savoury touch.
10. Bake the stuffed peppers in the preheated oven for about 25-30 minutes, or until the peppers are tender and the cheese is lightly browned.
11. Let the stuffed peppers rest for a few minutes before serving.
12. Serve the Diabetic Spinach and Feta Stuffed Peppers hot, garnished with fresh parsley if desired.

Nutritional Information (per serving):

- Calories: 150 kcal
- Carbohydrates: 10g
- Protein: 6g
- Fat: 8g
- Saturated Fat: 3g
- Fibre: 5g
- Sugar: 5g
- Sodium: 300mg

6. VEGETABLE CURRY WITH COCONUT MILK

Servings: 4
Prep time: 15 minutes
Cooking time: 25 minutes

Ingredients:

- 1 tablespoon vegetable oil
- 1 large onion, finely chopped
- 2 cloves garlic, minced
- 1 tablespoon grated ginger
- 1 red bell pepper, chopped
- 1 yellow bell pepper, chopped
- 1 small courgette (zucchini), chopped
- 200g cauliflower florets
- 100g green beans, trimmed and cut into bite-sized pieces
- 2 tablespoons curry powder
- 400ml sugar-free coconut milk
- 200ml vegetable broth (low-sodium)
- 1 tablespoon low-sodium soy sauce
- 1 tablespoon lime juice
- Salt and pepper to taste
- Fresh coriander leaves for garnish (optional)

Directions:

1. Heat the vegetable oil over medium heat in a large saucepan or wok. Add the finely chopped onion and sauté until it becomes soft and translucent.
2. Add the minced garlic and grated ginger to the pan, and cook for another minute until they become fragrant.
3. Stir in the chopped red and yellow bell peppers, courgette, cauliflower, and green beans. Cook for a few minutes until the vegetables start to soften.
4. Sprinkle the curry powder over the vegetables and toss everything together to coat the vegetables with the aromatic spice.
5. Pour in the sugar-free coconut milk and vegetable broth. Bring the mixture to a simmer and cook for about 15 minutes until the vegetables are tender and the curry sauce thickens.
6. Stir in the low-sodium soy sauce and lime juice. Season the Vegetable Curry with salt and pepper to taste.
7. Let the curry simmer for 2-3 minutes to allow the flavours to meld.
8. Serve the Diabetic Vegetable Curry with Coconut Milk hot, garnished with fresh coriander leaves if desired.

Nutritional Information (per serving):

- Calories: 250 kcal
- Carbohydrates: 15g
- Protein: 6g
- Fat: 15g
- Saturated Fat: 10g
- Fibre: 5g
- Sugar: 8g
- Sodium: 300mg

7. CAPRESE ZUCCHINI NOODLES

Servings: 2
Prep time: 15 minutes
Cooking time: 5 minutes

Ingredients:

- 2 medium zucchini
- 250g cherry tomatoes, halved
- 100g fresh mozzarella cheese, diced
- 2 tablespoons fresh basil leaves, torn
- 2 tablespoons extra-virgin olive oil
- 1 tablespoon balsamic vinegar
- 1 clove garlic, minced
- Salt and pepper to taste

Directions:

1. Wash the zucchini and trim off the ends. Use a spiralizer or a vegetable peeler to create zucchini noodles. If using a vegetable peeler, run it down the zucchini length to create thin ribbons. Set the zucchini noodles aside.
2. Combine the halved cherry tomatoes, diced fresh mozzarella cheese, and torn fresh basil leaves in a large mixing bowl.
3. Whisk together the extra-virgin olive oil, balsamic vinegar, minced garlic, salt, and pepper in a small bowl to create the dressing.
4. Pour the dressing over the tomato, mozzarella, and basil mixture. Toss everything together to coat the ingredients with the delicious sauce.
5. In a non-stick pan, heat the zucchini noodles over medium heat. Cook for 2-3 minutes, stirring occasionally, until the zucchini noodles are heated through but still tender-crisp. Be careful not to overcook them.
6. Remove the zucchini noodles from the pan and let them drain briefly on a paper towel to remove any excess moisture.
7. Add the warm zucchini noodles to the bowl with the tomato, mozzarella, and basil mixture. Toss everything gently to combine.
8. Divide the Diabetic Caprese Zucchini Noodles onto plates or bowls and serve immediately.

Nutritional Information (per serving):

- Calories: 250 kcal
- Carbohydrates: 10g
- Protein: 10g
- Fat: 18g
- Saturated Fat: 6g
- Fibre: 2g
- Sugar: 6g
- Sodium: 200mg

8. CHICKPEA AND VEGETABLE TAGINE

Servings: 4
Prep time: 15 minutes
Cooking time: 25 minutes

Ingredients:

- 1 tablespoon olive oil
- 1 large onion, finely chopped
- 2 cloves garlic, minced
- 1 teaspoon ground cumin
- 1 teaspoon ground coriander
- 1/2 teaspoon ground turmeric
- 1/4 teaspoon ground cinnamon
- 1/4 teaspoon cayenne pepper (optional for added spice)
- 2 large carrots, peeled and chopped
- 1 small sweet potato, peeled and chopped
- 400g canned chickpeas, drained and rinsed
- 400g canned chopped tomatoes
- 200ml vegetable broth (low-sodium)
- 50g dried apricots, chopped
- 50g pitted black olives
- Salt and pepper to taste
- Fresh coriander leaves for garnish (optional)
- Steamed couscous or quinoa for serving

Directions:

1. Heat the olive oil over medium heat in a large, deep frying pan or tagine. Add the finely chopped onion and sauté until it becomes soft and translucent.
2. Add the minced garlic to the pan and cook for another minute until it becomes fragrant.
3. Stir in the ground cumin, coriander, turmeric, cinnamon, and cayenne pepper (if using). Cook for a minute or two to toast the spices and release their flavours.
4. Add the chopped carrots and sweet potato to the pan. Cook for a few minutes to lightly brown the vegetables.
5. Stir in the drained and rinsed chickpeas, canned chopped tomatoes, and vegetable broth.
6. Add the chopped dried apricots and pitted black olives to the pan. These ingredients will add a touch of sweetness and tanginess to the dish.
7. Bring the mixture to a simmer and cook for about 20 minutes or until the carrots and sweet potatoes are tender.
8. Season the Chickpea and Vegetable Tagine with salt and pepper to taste.
9. Let the tagine simmer for a few minutes to allow the flavours to meld.
10. Serve the Diabetic Chickpea and Vegetable Tagine hot, garnished with fresh coriander leaves if desired. Accompany it with steamed couscous or quinoa for a complete and satisfying meal.

Nutritional Information (per serving, excluding couscous/quinoa):

- Calories: 300 kcal
- Carbohydrates: 50g
- Protein: 12g
- Fat: 6g
- Saturated Fat: 1g
- Fibre: 12g
- Sugar: 15g
- Sodium: 400mg

9. QUINOA STUFFED BELL PEPPERS

Servings: 4
Prep time: 20 minutes
Cooking time: 35 minutes

Ingredients:

- 4 large bell peppers (any colour), tops removed and seeds removed
- 250g quinoa, rinsed and drained
- 480ml vegetable broth (low-sodium)
- 1 tablespoon olive oil
- 1 small onion, finely chopped
- 2 cloves garlic, minced
- 1 carrot, finely diced
- 1 zucchini, finely diced
- 100g canned black beans, drained and rinsed
- 1 teaspoon ground cumin
- 1 teaspoon paprika
- 1/2 teaspoon dried oregano
- Salt and pepper to taste
- 100g grated cheddar cheese (or vegan cheese alternative)
- Fresh parsley for garnish (optional)

Directions:

1. Preheat the oven to 200°C (400°F).
2. In a saucepan, bring the vegetable broth to a boil. Add the rinsed quinoa, reduce the heat to low, cover, and let it simmer for about 15 minutes or until the quinoa is cooked and the liquid is absorbed. Fluff the quinoa with a fork and set it aside.
3. In a large frying pan, heat the olive oil over medium heat. Add the finely chopped onion and sauté until it becomes soft and translucent.
4. Add the minced garlic to the pan and cook for another minute until it becomes fragrant.
5. Stir in the finely diced carrot and zucchini. Cook for a few minutes until the vegetables start to soften.
6. Add the drained and rinsed black beans to the pan and cook for an additional 2 minutes to heat them through.
7. Sprinkle the ground cumin, paprika, dried oregano, salt, and pepper over the vegetable mixture. Stir everything together to evenly distribute the spices.
8. Combine the cooked quinoa with the seasoned vegetable mixture in a large mixing bowl. Mix well to incorporate all the ingredients.
9. Stuff each halved bell pepper with the quinoa and vegetable mixture. Press down gently to pack the stuffing.
10. Place the stuffed bell peppers on a baking tray or dish.
11. Sprinkle the grated cheddar cheese over the stuffed bell peppers.
12. Bake the stuffed peppers in the preheated oven for about 20 minutes or until the peppers are tender and the cheese is melted and slightly golden.
13. Let the stuffed peppers rest for a few minutes before serving.
14. Serve the Diabetic Quinoa Stuffed Bell Peppers hot, garnished with fresh parsley if desired.

Nutritional Information (per serving):

- Calories: 300 kcal
- Carbohydrates: 40g
- Protein: 12g
- Fat: 10g
- Saturated Fat: 4g
- Fibre: 8g
- Sugar: 5g
- Sodium: 350mg

10. SPINACH AND RICOTTA STUFFED SHELLS

Servings: 4
Prep time: 25 minutes
Cooking time: 30 minutes

Ingredients:

- 200g jumbo pasta shells (conchiglioni)
- 200g frozen chopped spinach, thawed and excess water squeezed out
- 250g ricotta cheese (low-fat, if available)
- 1 egg, lightly beaten
- 1/2 teaspoon dried oregano
- 1/2 teaspoon dried basil
- 1/4 teaspoon garlic powder
- Salt and pepper to taste
- 400ml sugar-free tomato sauce
- 50g grated Parmesan cheese
- Fresh basil leaves for garnish (optional)

Directions:

1. Preheat the oven to 190°C (375°F).
2. Cook the jumbo pasta shells according to the package instructions until they are al dente. Drain and set aside.
3. Combine the thawed and squeezed spinach, ricotta cheese, lightly beaten egg, dried oregano, dried basil, garlic powder, salt, and pepper in a mixing bowl. Mix everything thoroughly until well combined.
4. Spoon the spinach and ricotta mixture into each cooked jumbo pasta shell, gently pressing the filling to fill the shells completely.
5. Spread a thin layer of sugar-free tomato sauce in a baking dish to coat the bottom.
6. Arrange the stuffed shells in a single layer in the baking dish.
7. Pour the remaining tomato sauce over the stuffed shells, covering them evenly.
8. Sprinkle the grated Parmesan cheese over the top of the shells.
9. Cover the baking dish with foil and bake in the preheated oven for about 20 minutes.
10. Remove the foil and bake for an additional 10 minutes or until the cheese on top is melted and slightly golden.
11. Let the stuffed shells rest for a few minutes before serving.
12. Serve the Diabetic Spinach and Ricotta Stuffed Shells hot, garnished with fresh basil leaves if desired.

Nutritional Information (per serving):

- Calories: 350 kcal
- Carbohydrates: 35g
- Protein: 20g
- Fat: 15g
- Saturated Fat: 9g
- Fibre: 5g
- Sugar: 8g
- Sodium: 400mg

11. TOFU AND VEGETABLE STIR-FRY

Servings: 4
Prep time: 20 minutes
Cooking time: 15 minutes

Ingredients:

- 300g firm tofu, drained and cubed
- 2 tablespoons low-sodium soy sauce
- 2 tablespoons cornstarch
- 2 tablespoons vegetable oil
- 1 red bell pepper, sliced
- 1 yellow bell pepper, sliced
- 1 carrot, sliced
- 100g green beans, trimmed and halved
- 1 small broccoli head, florets separated
- 2 cloves garlic, minced
- 1 teaspoon grated ginger
- 2 tablespoons low-sodium vegetable broth
- 1 tablespoon rice vinegar
- 1 tablespoon hoisin sauce (sugar-free if available)
- 1/2 teaspoon sesame oil
- Salt and pepper to taste
- Sesame seeds and sliced spring onions for garnish (optional)
- Steamed brown rice for serving

Directions:

1. In a bowl, toss the cubed tofu with low-sodium soy sauce. Sprinkle cornstarch over the tofu and toss again until the tofu cubes are coated. Set aside.
2. Heat 1 tablespoon of vegetable oil over medium-high heat in a wok or large frying pan. Add the marinated tofu cubes to the wok and cook until golden and slightly crispy. Remove the tofu from the wok and set aside.
3. In the same wok, add the remaining 1 tablespoon of vegetable oil. Stir-fry the sliced red and yellow bell peppers, carrot, and green beans for a few minutes until they start to soften.
4. Add the broccoli florets to the wok and stir until all the vegetables are tender-crisp.
5. Push the vegetables to one side of the wok and add the minced garlic and grated ginger to the open space. Cook for a minute or until they become fragrant.
6. Mix the garlic and ginger with the vegetables in the wok.
7. Whisk together the low-sodium vegetable broth, rice vinegar, hoisin sauce, and sesame oil in a small bowl to make the sauce.
8. Pour the sauce over the vegetables in the wok and toss everything together to coat the vegetables in the delicious sauce.
9. Return the cooked tofu cubes to the wok and gently stir-fry to combine with the vegetables and sauce.
10. Season the Tofu and Vegetable Stir-Fry with salt and pepper to taste.
11. Serve the Diabetic Tofu and Vegetable Stir-Fry hot, garnished with sesame seeds and sliced spring onions if desired. Accompany it with steamed brown rice for a complete and satisfying meal.

Nutritional Information (per serving, excluding rice):

- Calories: 250 kcal
- Carbohydrates: 15g
- Protein: 12g
- Fat: 15g
- Saturated Fat: 2g
- Fibre: 5g
- Sugar: 6g
- Sodium: 400mg

12. MEDITERRANEAN VEGETABLE AND FETA QUICHE

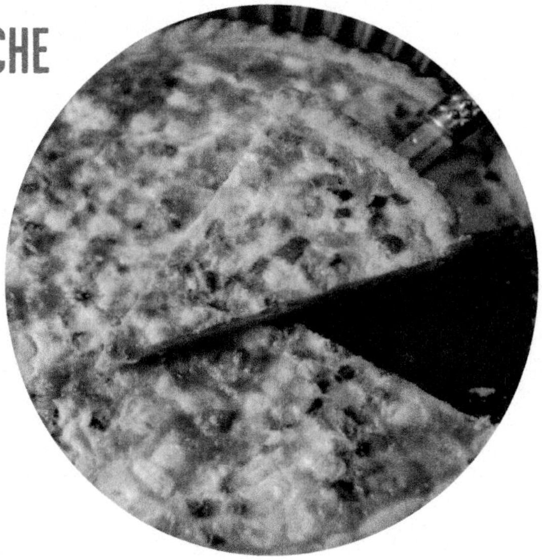

Servings: 6
Prep time: 25 minutes
Cooking time: 40 minutes

Ingredients:

- 1 ready-made whole-grain pie crust (9-inch)
- 1 tablespoon olive oil
- 1 small red onion, finely chopped
- 1 red bell pepper, diced
- 1 zucchini, diced
- 100g cherry tomatoes, halved
- 50g baby spinach leaves
- 4 large eggs
- 200ml low-fat milk
- 100g crumbled feta cheese
- 1 teaspoon dried oregano
- Salt and pepper to taste

Directions:

1. Preheat the oven to 190°C (375°F).
2. In a large frying pan, heat the olive oil over medium heat. Add the finely chopped red onion and sauté until it becomes soft and translucent.
3. Add the diced red bell pepper and zucchini to the pan. Cook for a few minutes until the vegetables start to soften.
4. Stir in the halved cherry tomatoes and baby spinach leaves. Cook for an additional 2 minutes until the spinach wilts and the tomatoes are slightly softened.
5. Remove the pan from the heat and set aside.
6. Whisk together the eggs and low-fat milk in a separate bowl until well combined.
7. Add the crumbled feta cheese to the egg mixture and stir to distribute the cheese evenly.
8. Season the egg mixture with dried oregano, salt, and pepper to taste.
9. Place the ready-made whole-grain pie crust in a pie dish.
10. Spread the sautéed vegetable mixture evenly over the pie crust.
11. Pour the seasoned egg and feta mixture over the vegetables in the pie crust, ensuring an even distribution.
12. Carefully place the quiche in the preheated oven and bake for about 35-40 minutes until the top is golden and the quiche is set in the centre.
13. Remove the quiche from the oven and let it cool for a few minutes before slicing and serving.
14. Serve the Diabetic Mediterranean Vegetable and Feta Quiche warm or at room temperature.

Nutritional Information (per serving):

- Calories: 250 kcal
- Carbohydrates: 20g
- Protein: 12g
- Fat: 12g
- Saturated Fat: 5g
- Fibre: 3g
- Sugar: 4g
- Sodium: 350mg

CHAPTER 6

SALADS

1. GREEK SALAD

Servings: 4
Prep time: 15 minutes
Cooking time: 0 minutes

Ingredients:

- 2 large ripe tomatoes, diced
- 1 cucumber, peeled and diced
- 1 red bell pepper, diced
- 1/2 red onion, thinly sliced
- 100g black olives, pitted and halved
- 100g crumbled feta cheese (low-fat, if available)
- 2 tablespoons extra-virgin olive oil
- 1 tablespoon red wine vinegar
- 1 teaspoon dried oregano
- Salt and pepper to taste
- Fresh parsley for garnish (optional)

Directions:

1. In a large salad bowl, combine the diced tomatoes, cucumber, red bell pepper, thinly sliced red onion, and halved black olives.
2. Whisk together the extra-virgin olive oil, red wine vinegar, dried oregano, salt, and pepper in a small bowl to make the dressing.
3. Pour the dressing over the vegetables in the salad bowl.
4. Gently toss all the ingredients together to coat the vegetables with the dressing.
5. Sprinkle the crumbled feta cheese over the salad.
6. Garnish the Diabetic Greek Salad with fresh parsley if desired.
7. Serve the salad immediately as a refreshing and healthy side dish.

Nutritional Information (per serving):

- Calories: 180 kcal
- Carbohydrates: 10g
- Protein: 5g
- Fat: 14g
- Saturated Fat: 4g
- Fibre: 3g
- Sugar: 5g
- Sodium: 400mg

2. CAPRESE SALAD

Servings: 4
Prep time: 10 minutes
Cooking time: 0 minutes

Ingredients:

- 4 large ripe tomatoes, sliced
- 200g fresh mozzarella cheese, sliced
- Fresh basil leaves
- 2 tablespoons extra-virgin olive oil
- 1 tablespoon balsamic vinegar (sugar-free if available)
- Salt and pepper to taste

Directions:

1. Arrange the sliced tomatoes and fresh mozzarella cheese on a serving platter in alternating layers.
2. Tuck fresh basil leaves between the tomato and mozzarella slices.
3. Whisk together the extra-virgin olive oil, balsamic vinegar, salt, and pepper in a small bowl to make the dressing.
4. Drizzle the dressing over the Caprese Salad.
5. Garnish the salad with additional fresh basil leaves if desired.
6. Serve the Diabetic Caprese Salad immediately as a light, refreshing appetizer or side dish.

Nutritional Information (per serving):

- Calories: 200 kcal
- Carbohydrates: 5g
- Protein: 10g
- Fat: 15g
- Saturated Fat: 6g
- Fibre: 1g
- Sugar: 4g
- Sodium: 300mg

3.QUINOA AND CHICKPEA SALAD

Servings: 4
Prep time: 15 minutes
Cooking time: 15 minutes

Ingredients:

- 250g quinoa
- 400g canned chickpeas, drained and rinsed
- 1 red bell pepper, diced
- 1 cucumber, diced
- 1/4 red onion, finely chopped
- 50g baby spinach leaves
- 2 tablespoons chopped fresh parsley
- 2 tablespoons chopped fresh mint
- 2 tablespoons extra-virgin olive oil
- 1 tablespoon lemon juice
- 1 teaspoon Dijon mustard
- Salt and pepper to taste

Directions:

1. Rinse the quinoa under cold water in a fine-mesh sieve. In a saucepan, add the rinsed quinoa and 480ml of water. Bring to a boil, then reduce the heat to low and simmer for 12-15 minutes or until the quinoa is cooked and the water is absorbed. Fluff the quinoa with a fork and let it cool.
2. In a large salad bowl, combine the cooked quinoa, drained and rinsed chickpeas, diced red bell pepper, diced cucumber, finely chopped red onion, baby spinach leaves, chopped fresh parsley, and chopped fresh mint.
3. Whisk together the extra-virgin olive oil, lemon juice, Dijon mustard, salt, and pepper in a small bowl to make the dressing.
4. Pour the dressing over the quinoa and chickpea mixture.
5. Gently toss all the ingredients together to coat the salad with the dressing.
6. Adjust salt and pepper to taste.
7. Serve the Diabetic Quinoa and Chickpea Salad chilled as a hearty and nutritious main course or side dish.

Nutritional Information (per serving):

- Calories: 300 kcal
- Carbohydrates: 40g
- Protein: 10g
- Fat: 12g
- Saturated Fat: 2g
- Fibre: 8g
- Sugar: 5g
- Sodium: 300mg

4. ROASTED VEGETABLE SALAD

Servings: 4
Prep time: 15 minutes
Cooking time: 25 minutes

Ingredients:

- 500g mixed vegetables (e.g. bell peppers, zucchini, cherry tomatoes, red onions, and broccoli), chopped
- 2 tablespoons extra-virgin olive oil
- 1 teaspoon dried thyme
- 1 teaspoon dried rosemary
- 1/2 teaspoon garlic powder
- Salt and pepper to taste
- 100g mixed salad greens (e.g. spinach, rocket, and lettuce)
- 50g crumbled feta cheese (low-fat, if available)
- 2 tablespoons balsamic vinegar (sugar-free if available)

Directions:

1. Preheat the oven to 200°C (390°F).
2. In a large bowl, toss the chopped mixed vegetables with extra-virgin olive oil, dried thyme, dried rosemary, garlic powder, salt, and pepper until the vegetables are well coated.
3. Spread the seasoned vegetables in a single layer on a baking sheet lined with parchment paper.
4. Roast the vegetables in the preheated oven for about 25 minutes or until they are tender and slightly caramelized, stirring halfway through.
5. While the vegetables are roasting, prepare the salad greens by washing and drying them thoroughly.
6. In a serving bowl, arrange the mixed salad greens.
7. Once the roasted vegetables are done, remove them from the oven and let them cool slightly.
8. Place the roasted vegetables on top of the mixed salad greens in the serving bowl.
9. Sprinkle the crumbled feta cheese over the salad.
10. Drizzle the balsamic vinegar over the salad as a light and tangy dressing.
11. Gently toss all the ingredients together to combine the roasted vegetables, salad greens, and feta cheese.
12. Adjust salt and pepper to taste.
13. Serve the Diabetic Roasted Vegetable Salad as a wholesome and nutritious main course or side dish.

Nutritional Information (per serving):

- Calories: 180 kcal
- Carbohydrates: 15g
- Protein: 6g
- Fat: 12g
- Saturated Fat: 4g
- Fibre: 5g
- Sugar: 6g
- Sodium: 250mg

5. AVOCADO AND SHRIMP SALAD

Servings: 4
Prep time: 15 minutes
Cooking time: 5 minutes

Ingredients:

- 400g cooked shrimp, peeled and deveined
- 2 ripe avocados, peeled, pitted, and diced
- 250g cherry tomatoes, halved
- 1/4 red onion, finely chopped
- 50g mixed salad greens (e.g. spinach, rocket, and lettuce)
- 2 tablespoons chopped fresh cilantro (coriander)
- 2 tablespoons extra-virgin olive oil
- 1 tablespoon lemon juice
- 1 teaspoon Dijon mustard
- Salt and pepper to taste

Directions:

1. Combine the cooked shrimp, diced avocados, halved cherry tomatoes, finely chopped red onion, mixed salad greens, and chopped fresh cilantro in a large salad bowl.
2. Whisk together the extra-virgin olive oil, lemon juice, Dijon mustard, salt, and pepper in a small bowl to make the dressing.
3. Pour the dressing over the Avocado and Shrimp Salad.
4. Gently toss all the ingredients together to coat the salad with the dressing.
5. Adjust salt and pepper to taste.
6. Serve the Diabetic Avocado and Shrimp Salad as a refreshing and nutritious main course or appetizer.

Nutritional Information (per serving):

- Calories: 250 kcal
- Carbohydrates: 10g
- Protein: 20g
- Fat: 15g
- Saturated Fat: 2g
- Fibre: 6g
- Sugar: 2g
- Sodium: 300mg

6. TOFU AND BROCCOLI SALAD

Servings: 4
Prep time: 15 minutes
Cooking time: 10 minutes

Ingredients:

- 400g firm tofu, drained and cubed
- 200g broccoli florets
- 1 red bell pepper, thinly sliced
- 1 carrot, peeled and grated
- 50g mixed salad greens (e.g. spinach, rocket, and lettuce)
- 2 tablespoons chopped fresh coriander (cilantro)
- 2 tablespoons extra-virgin olive oil
- 1 tablespoon soy sauce (reduced sodium if available)
- 1 tablespoon rice vinegar
- 1 teaspoon grated fresh ginger
- 1 clove garlic, minced
- Salt and pepper to taste
- 1 tablespoon sesame seeds for garnish (optional)

Directions:

1. Heat 1 tablespoon of olive oil over medium heat in a large pan. Add the cubed tofu and cook for about 5-7 minutes, or until the tofu turns golden brown and crispy on all sides. Remove the tofu from the pan and set aside.
2. In the same pan, add the broccoli florets and cook for about 3-4 minutes or until they are tender-crisp. Remove the broccoli from the pan and set aside.
3. Combine the cooked tofu, broccoli florets, thinly sliced red bell pepper, grated carrot, mixed salad greens, and chopped fresh coriander in a large salad bowl.
4. In a small bowl, whisk together the remaining 1 tablespoon of olive oil, soy sauce, rice vinegar, grated fresh ginger, minced garlic, salt, and pepper to make the dressing.
5. Pour the dressing over the Tofu and Broccoli Salad.
6. Gently toss all the ingredients together to coat the salad with the dressing.
7. Adjust salt and pepper to taste.
8. Garnish the salad with sesame seeds, if desired.
9. Serve the Diabetic Tofu and Broccoli Salad as a nutritious and flavourful main course or side dish.

Nutritional Information (per serving):

- Calories: 220 kcal
- Carbohydrates: 10g
- Protein: 12g
- Fat: 15g
- Saturated Fat: 2g
- Fibre: 4g
- Sugar: 3g
- Sodium: 200mg

7. BEET AND GOAT CHEESE SALAD

Servings: 4
Prep time: 15 minutes
Cooking time: 45 minutes

Ingredients:

- 4 medium beets, peeled and cubed
- 100g mixed salad greens (e.g. spinach, rocket, and lettuce)
- 75g goat cheese, crumbled
- 50g walnuts, chopped
- 2 tablespoons extra-virgin olive oil
- 1 tablespoon balsamic vinegar (sugar-free if available)
- 1 teaspoon Dijon mustard
- Salt and pepper to taste

Directions:

1. Preheat the oven to 200°C (390°F).
2. In a baking dish, toss the cubed beets with 1 tablespoon of olive oil, salt, and pepper until the beets are well coated.
3. Roast the beets in the preheated oven for about 45 minutes or until they are tender when pierced with a fork.
4. While the beets are roasting, prepare the salad greens by washing and drying them thoroughly.
5. Combine the roasted beets, mixed salad greens, crumbled goat cheese, and chopped walnuts in a large salad bowl.
6. Whisk together the remaining 1 tablespoon of olive oil, balsamic vinegar, Dijon mustard, salt, and pepper in a small bowl to make the dressing.
7. Pour the dressing over the Beet and Goat Cheese Salad.
8. Gently toss all the ingredients together to coat the salad with the dressing.
9. Adjust salt and pepper to taste.
10. Serve the Diabetic Beet and Goat Cheese Salad as a delightful and nutritious main course or side dish.

Nutritional Information (per serving):

- Calories: 250 kcal
- Carbohydrates: 15g
- Protein: 8g
- Fat: 18g
- Saturated Fat: 5g
- Fibre: 4g
- Sugar: 10g
- Sodium: 200mg

8. WALDORF SALAD

Servings: 4
Prep time: 15 minutes

Ingredients:

- 2 medium apples, cored and diced
- 2 celery stalks, thinly sliced
- 50g walnuts, chopped
- 50g seedless grapes, halved
- 50g mixed salad greens (e.g. spinach, rocket, and lettuce)
- 100g plain Greek yoghurt (sugar-free if available)
- 1 tablespoon lemon juice
- 1 teaspoon honey (optional, or use a sugar-free alternative)
- 1/2 teaspoon ground cinnamon
- Salt and pepper to taste

Directions:

1. Combine the diced apples, thinly sliced celery, chopped walnuts, halved grapes, and mixed salad greens in a large salad bowl.
2. In a small bowl, whisk together the plain Greek yoghurt, lemon juice, honey (if using), ground cinnamon, salt, and pepper to make the dressing.
3. Pour the dressing over the Waldorf Salad.
4. Gently toss all the ingredients together to coat the salad with the dressing.
5. Adjust salt, pepper, and sweetness to taste.
6. Serve the Diabetic Waldorf Salad as a refreshing and nutritious main course or side dish.

Nutritional Information (per serving):

- Calories: 200 kcal
- Carbohydrates: 20g
- Protein: 6g
- Fat: 10g
- Saturated Fat: 1g
- Fibre: 4g
- Sugar: 12g
- Sodium: 60mg

CHAPTER 7

SAUCES, DRESSINGS, AND CONDIMENTS

1. TOMATO BASIL SAUCE

Servings: 2 cups
Prep time: 10 minutes
Cooking time: 25 minutes

Ingredients:

- 800g fresh tomatoes, diced (or 2 cans of diced tomatoes)
- 1 small onion, finely chopped
- 2 cloves garlic, minced
- 2 tablespoons extra-virgin olive oil
- 1 tablespoon tomato paste
- 1 teaspoon dried basil
- 1/2 teaspoon dried oregano
- 1/2 teaspoon dried thyme
- Salt and pepper to taste

Directions:

1. In a large saucepan, heat the extra-virgin olive oil over medium heat. Add the finely chopped onion and minced garlic. Sauté for about 2-3 minutes until the onion becomes translucent and the garlic is fragrant.
2. Add the diced tomatoes (or canned tomatoes) to the saucepan and the tomato paste, dried basil, dried oregano, dried thyme, salt, and pepper. Stir well to combine all the ingredients.
3. Bring the mixture to a simmer, then reduce the heat to low. Cover the saucepan and let the sauce cook for about 20 minutes, stirring occasionally to prevent sticking.
4. After 20 minutes, the tomatoes should have softened, and the sauce should have thickened slightly.
5. Gently mash the tomatoes to achieve your desired consistency using a potato masher or a fork. If you prefer a smoother sauce, use an immersion blender to puree the sauce.
6. Taste the sauce and adjust the seasoning with more salt and pepper if needed.
7. Continue to cook the sauce uncovered for another 5 minutes to allow the flavours to meld.
8. Remove the saucepan from the heat and let the Tomato Basil Sauce cool slightly.
9. Serve the Diabetic Tomato Basil Sauce over your favourite low-carb pasta or zucchini noodles, and enjoy!

Nutritional Information (per serving - 1/4 cup):

- Calories: 50 kcal
- Carbohydrates: 7g
- Protein: 1g
- Fat: 3g
- Saturated Fat: 0.4g
- Fibre: 2g
- Sugar: 4g
- Sodium: 100mg

2. ROASTED RED PEPPER SAUCE

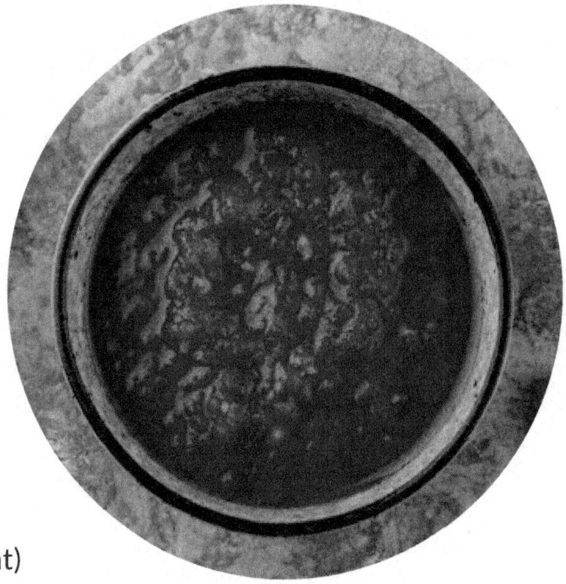

Servings: 2 cups
Prep time: 10 minutes
Cooking time: 20 minutes

Ingredients:

- 4 large red bell peppers
- 1 small onion, finely chopped
- 2 cloves garlic, minced
- 2 tablespoons extra-virgin olive oil
- 1 teaspoon dried basil
- 1/2 teaspoon dried oregano
- 1/4 teaspoon dried chilli flakes (optional for added heat)
- Salt and pepper to taste

Directions:

1. Preheat the oven to 200°C (390°F).
2. Wash the red bell peppers and pat them dry. Place the whole peppers on a baking sheet lined with parchment paper.
3. Roast the red bell peppers in the preheated oven for about 15-20 minutes, turning them occasionally, until the skins are charred and blistered.
4. Remove the peppers from the oven and transfer them to a heatproof bowl. Cover the bowl with plastic wrap or a lid to allow the peppers to steam for about 10 minutes.
5. After steaming, peel off the charred skins from the roasted red peppers and discard them. Cut the peppers in half, remove the seeds and stems, and roughly chop the flesh.
6. In a saucepan, heat the extra-virgin olive oil over medium heat. Add the finely chopped onion and minced garlic. Sauté for 2-3 minutes until the onion becomes translucent and the garlic is fragrant.
7. Add the chopped roasted red peppers to the saucepan and the dried basil, dried oregano, dried chilli flakes (if using), salt, and pepper. Stir well to combine all the ingredients.
8. Bring the mixture to a simmer, then reduce the heat to low. Cover the saucepan and let the sauce cook for about 5 minutes, stirring occasionally.
9. After 5 minutes, the flavours should have melded together.
10. Using an immersion or regular blender, puree the sauce until smooth and creamy.
11. Taste the sauce and adjust the seasoning with more salt and pepper if needed.
12. Continue to cook the sauce uncovered for another 5 minutes to thicken it slightly.
13. Remove the saucepan from the heat and let the Roasted Red Pepper Sauce cool slightly.
14. Serve the Diabetic Roasted Red Pepper Sauce over grilled chicken, fish, or your favourite low-carb pasta, and enjoy!

Nutritional Information (per serving - 1/4 cup):

- Calories: 50 kcal
- Carbohydrates: 4g
- Protein: 1g
- Fat: 4g
- Saturated Fat: 0.5g
- Fibre: 1g
- Sugar: 2g
- Sodium: 150mg

3. GARLIC AND HERB MARINADE

Servings: 1 cup
Prep time: 10 minutes
Cooking time: 0 minutes

Ingredients:

- 4 cloves garlic, minced
- 75g fresh parsley, finely chopped
- 2 tablespoons fresh basil, finely chopped
- 2 tablespoons fresh rosemary, finely chopped
- 75g extra-virgin olive oil
- 1 tablespoon balsamic vinegar
- 1 teaspoon Dijon mustard
- 1/2 teaspoon dried oregano
- 1/2 teaspoon dried thyme
- Salt and pepper to taste

Directions:

1. Combine the minced garlic, finely chopped parsley, basil, and rosemary in a mixing bowl.
2. Add the extra-virgin olive oil, balsamic vinegar, Dijon mustard, oregano, thyme, salt, and pepper to the bowl.
3. Stir well to blend all the ingredients and create the Garlic and Herb Marinade.
4. Taste the marinade and adjust the seasoning with more salt and pepper if needed.
5. Use the marinade immediately to marinate your preferred protein, such as chicken, fish, or tofu. Alternatively, transfer the marinade to an airtight container and store it in the refrigerator for up to 5 days.
6. Place your protein in a shallow dish or a resealable plastic bag to use the marinade. Pour the marinade over the protein, making sure it is coated evenly. Seal the dish or bag and refrigerate for at least 30 minutes, or ideally overnight, to allow the flavours to infuse.
7. After marinating, cook your protein as desired, whether grilling, roasting, or pan-searing.

Nutritional Information (per serving - 1 tablespoon):

- Calories: 50 kcal
- Carbohydrates: 1g
- Protein: 0.2g
- Fat: 5g
- Saturated Fat: 0.7g
- Fibre: 0.2g
- Sugar: 0.1g
- Sodium: 25mg

4. LEMON DILL SAUCE

Servings: 1 cup
Prep time: 5 minutes
Cooking time: 0 minutes

Ingredients:

- 120ml plain Greek yoghurt (sugar-free if available)
- 2 tablespoons fresh dill, finely chopped
- Zest of 1 lemon
- 2 tablespoons lemon juice
- 1 clove garlic, minced
- 1/2 teaspoon Dijon mustard
- Salt and pepper to taste

Directions:

1. Combine the plain Greek yoghurt, finely chopped dill, lemon zest, lemon juice, minced garlic, and Dijon mustard in a mixing bowl.
2. Stir well to blend all the ingredients and create the Lemon Dill Sauce.
3. Taste the sauce and adjust the seasoning with salt and pepper.
4. Use the Lemon Dill Sauce immediately as a refreshing and tangy accompaniment to grilled fish, chicken, or vegetables. Alternatively, transfer the sauce to an airtight container and store it in the refrigerator for up to 3 days.
5. Serve the Diabetic Lemon Dill Sauce drizzled over your favourite protein or as a delightful vegetable dipping sauce.

Nutritional Information (per serving - 1 tablespoon):

- Calories: 10 kcal
- Carbohydrates: 1g
- Protein: 1g
- Fat: 0.4g
- Saturated Fat: 0.1g
- Fibre: 0g
- Sugar: 0.6g
- Sodium: 15mg

5. TERIYAKI GLAZE

Servings: 1/2 cup
Prep time: 5 minutes
Cooking time: 10 minutes

Ingredients:

- 120ml reduced-sodium soy sauce
- 60ml water
- 2 tablespoons erythritol (or your preferred sugar substitute)
- 1 tablespoon rice vinegar
- 1 clove garlic, minced
- 1 teaspoon grated fresh ginger
- 1 teaspoon cornstarch (or arrowroot powder for a gluten-free option)
- 1 tablespoon water

Directions:

1. Combine the reduced-sodium soy sauce, water, erythritol (or your preferred sugar substitute), rice vinegar, minced garlic, and grated fresh ginger in a small saucepan.
2. Place the saucepan over medium heat and bring the mixture to a simmer.
3. Mix the cornstarch (or arrowroot powder) in a separate small bowl with 1 tablespoon of water to create a slurry.
4. Gradually pour the cornstarch slurry into the simmering sauce while stirring continuously. This will help thicken the glaze.
5. Continue to cook the sauce for about 5 minutes, stirring occasionally, until it reaches a glossy and slightly thickened consistency.
6. Remove the saucepan from the heat and let the Teriyaki Glaze cool slightly.
7. Use the Diabetic Teriyaki Glaze immediately as a delicious and savoury glaze for grilled chicken, salmon, tofu, or vegetables. Alternatively, transfer the glaze to an airtight container and store it in the refrigerator for up to 5 days.
8. Brush the Teriyaki Glaze over your preferred protein or vegetables during the last few minutes of cooking or grilling to achieve a delicious caramelized finish.

Nutritional Information (per serving - 1 tablespoon):

- Calories: 10 kcal
- Carbohydrates: 2g
- Protein: 0.5g
- Fat: 0g
- Saturated Fat: 0g
- Fibre: 0g
- Sugar: 0.5g
- Sodium: 250mg

6. BALSAMIC VINAIGRETTE

Servings: 1/2 cup
Prep time: 5 minutes
Cooking time: 0 minutes

Ingredients:

- 60ml balsamic vinegar
- 60ml extra-virgin olive oil
- 1 tablespoon Dijon mustard
- 1 clove garlic, minced
- 1 teaspoon dried oregano
- 1/2 teaspoon dried basil
- Salt and pepper to taste

Directions:

1. Combine the balsamic vinegar, extra-virgin olive oil, Dijon mustard, minced garlic, dried oregano, and dried basil in a small bowl.
2. Whisk the ingredients together until the vinaigrette is well emulsified and the oil and vinegar thoroughly blend.
3. Taste the vinaigrette and season with salt and pepper according to your preference.
4. Use the Diabetic Balsamic Vinaigrette immediately as a tangy and flavorful dressing for salads or grilled vegetables. Alternatively, transfer the vinaigrette to an airtight container and store it in the refrigerator for up to 5 days.
5. Drizzle the Balsamic Vinaigrette over your salad just before serving to enjoy its delightful taste.

Nutritional Information (per serving - 1 tablespoon):

- Calories: 70 kcal
- Carbohydrates: 1g
- Protein: 0g
- Fat: 7g
- Saturated Fat: 1g
- Fibre: 0g
- Sugar: 0g
- Sodium: 40mg

7. LEMON HERB DRESSING

Servings: 1/2 cup
Prep time: 5 minutes
Cooking time: 0 minutes

Ingredients:

- Juice of 1 lemon
- Zest of 1 lemon
- 60ml extra-virgin olive oil
- 2 tablespoons fresh parsley, finely chopped
- 1 tablespoon fresh basil, finely chopped
- 1 teaspoon fresh thyme leaves
- 1 clove garlic, minced
- Salt and pepper to taste

Directions:

1. Combine the lemon juice, lemon zest, extra-virgin olive oil, finely chopped parsley, basil, and thyme leaves in a small bowl.
2. Add the minced garlic to the bowl.
3. Whisk all ingredients until the Lemon Herb Dressing is combined and emulsified.
4. Taste the dressing and season with salt and pepper according to your preference.
5. Use the Diabetic Lemon Herb Dressing immediately as a zesty and aromatic salad dressing or drizzled over grilled fish, chicken, or vegetables. Alternatively, transfer the dressing to an airtight container and store it in the refrigerator for up to 5 days.
6. Drizzle the Lemon Herb Dressing over your salad just before serving, or use it as a marinade for your favourite proteins for added flavour.

Nutritional Information (per serving - 1 tablespoon):

- Calories: 50 kcal
- Carbohydrates: 1g
- Protein: 0g
- Fat: 5g
- Saturated Fat: 0.7g
- Fibre: 0g
- Sugar: 0g
- Sodium: 0mg

8. GREEK YOGURT RANCH DRESSING

Servings: 1 cup
Prep time: 10 minutes
Cooking time: 0 minutes

Ingredients:

- 250ml plain Greek yoghurt (sugar-free if available)
- 2 tablespoons fresh chives, finely chopped
- 1 tablespoon fresh dill, finely chopped
- 1 clove garlic, minced
- 1 teaspoon onion powder
- 1 teaspoon dried parsley
- 1/2 teaspoon dried dill
- 1/4 teaspoon paprika
- 1 tablespoon lemon juice
- 1 tablespoon white vinegar
- Salt and pepper to taste

Directions:

1. Combine the plain Greek yoghurt, finely chopped chives, dill, and minced garlic in a mixing bowl.
2. Add the onion powder, dried parsley, dill, and paprika to the bowl.
3. Mix all the ingredients until well combined, and the herbs are evenly distributed throughout the Greek yoghurt.
4. Stir in the lemon juice and white vinegar to enhance the tangy flavour of the dressing.
5. Taste the dressing and season with salt and pepper according to your preference.
6. Use the Diabetic Greek Yogurt Ranch Dressing immediately as a creamy and flavorful dressing for salads, vegetable dips, or drizzled-over grilled chicken or fish. Alternatively, transfer the sauce to an airtight container and store it in the refrigerator for up to 5 days.
7. Serve the dressing as a healthier alternative to traditional ranch dressing, providing a creamy and tangy taste to your favourite dishes.

Nutritional Information (per serving - 1 tablespoon):

- Calories: 10 kcal
- Carbohydrates: 1g
- Protein: 1g
- Fat: 0.3g
- Saturated Fat: 0.1g
- Fibre: 0g
- Sugar: 0.5g
- Sodium: 10mg

9. Apple Cider Vinaigrette

Servings: 3/4 cup
Prep time: 5 minutes
Cooking time: 0 minutes

Ingredients:

- 120ml apple cider vinegar
- 60ml extra-virgin olive oil
- 2 tablespoons apple cider (sugar-free if available)
- 1 tablespoon Dijon mustard
- 1 clove garlic, minced
- 1/2 teaspoon dried oregano
- 1/2 teaspoon dried thyme
- Salt and pepper to taste

Directions:

1. Combine the apple cider vinegar, extra-virgin olive oil, apple cider, Dijon mustard, and minced garlic in a small bowl.
2. Add the dried oregano and dried thyme to the bowl.
3. Whisk all the ingredients together until the Apple Cider Vinaigrette is well emulsified and the oil and vinegar are thoroughly blended.
4. Taste the vinaigrette and season with salt and pepper according to your preference.
5. Use the Diabetic Apple Cider Vinaigrette immediately as a tangy and sweet salad dressing or as a grilled chicken or fish marinade. Alternatively, transfer the vinaigrette to an airtight container and store it in the refrigerator for up to 5 days.
6. Drizzle the Apple Cider Vinaigrette over your salad just before serving to enjoy its delightful taste.

Nutritional Information (per serving - 1 tablespoon):

- Calories: 40 kcal
- Carbohydrates: 1g
- Protein: 0g
- Fat: 4g
- Saturated Fat: 0.6g
- Fibre: 0g
- Sugar: 0.5g
- Sodium: 10mg

10. SESAME GINGER DRESSING

Servings: 1/2 cup
Prep time: 10 minutes
Cooking time: 0 minutes

Ingredients:

- 60ml reduced-sodium soy sauce
- 2 tablespoons rice vinegar
- 1 tablespoon sesame oil
- 1 tablespoon fresh ginger, grated
- 1 clove garlic, minced
- 1 teaspoon erythritol (or your preferred sugar substitute)
- 1 tablespoon water
- 1 teaspoon sesame seeds (optional)
- Salt and pepper to taste

Directions:

1. Combine the reduced-sodium soy sauce, rice vinegar, sesame oil, grated ginger, and minced garlic in a small bowl.
2. Add the erythritol (or your preferred sugar substitute) to the bowl.
3. Mix the sesame seeds (if using) in a separate small bowl with 1 tablespoon of water.
4. Gradually pour the sesame seed mixture into the dressing while stirring continuously. This will add a nutty flavour to the sauce.
5. Season the dressing with salt and pepper according to your preference.
6. Use the Diabetic Sesame Ginger Dressing immediately as a savoury and tangy salad dressing or as a stir-fries and grilled proteins marinade. Alternatively, transfer the dressing to an airtight container and store it in the refrigerator for up to 5 days.
7. Drizzle the Sesame Ginger Dressing over your salad, or use it to enhance the flavour of your favourite dishes.

Nutritional Information (per serving - 1 tablespoon):

- Calories: 15 kcal
- Carbohydrates: 1g
- Protein: 1g
- Fat: 1g
- Saturated Fat: 0g
- Fibre: 0g
- Sugar: 0g
- Sodium: 150mg

11. GUACAMOLE

Servings: 1 cup
Prep time: 10 minutes
Cooking time: 0 minutes

Ingredients:

- 2 ripe avocados
- 1 small tomato, diced
- 75g red onion, finely chopped
- 1 clove garlic, minced
- 1 tablespoon fresh lime juice
- 1 tablespoon fresh cilantro, chopped
- 1/2 teaspoon ground cumin
- Salt and pepper to taste

Directions:

1. Cut the avocados in half, remove the seeds, and scoop the flesh into a mixing bowl.
2. Mash the avocado with a fork or potato masher until it reaches your desired consistency. Some prefer it chunky, while others like it smooth.
3. Add the diced tomato, finely chopped red onion, and minced garlic to the mashed avocado.
4. Stir in the fresh lime juice, chopped cilantro, and ground cumin to enhance the flavours.
5. Season the guacamole with salt and pepper according to your preference.
6. Mix all the ingredients until well combined and the flavours are evenly distributed.
7. Use the Diabetic Guacamole immediately as a creamy and flavorful dip for vegetable sticks and whole-grain crackers, or as a topping for grilled chicken or fish. Alternatively, transfer the guacamole to an airtight container and store it in the refrigerator for up to 2 days.
8. Serve the guacamole as a delicious and diabetes-friendly snack or appetizer, offering healthy fats and essential nutrients.

Nutritional Information (per serving - 2 tablespoons):

- Calories: 50 kcal
- Carbohydrates: 3g
- Protein: 1g
- Fat: 4g
- Saturated Fat: 0.7g
- Fibre: 2g
- Sugar: 0.5g
- Sodium: 40mg

12. SALSA VERDE

Servings: 1 cup
Prep time: 10 minutes
Cooking time: 0 minutes

Ingredients:

- 250g fresh parsley, chopped
- 75g fresh cilantro, chopped
- 75g fresh mint leaves, chopped
- 1 clove garlic, minced
- 75g red onion, finely chopped
- 1 tablespoon fresh lime juice
- 1 tablespoon white vinegar
- 1 tablespoon olive oil
- 1/4 teaspoon ground cumin
- Salt and pepper to taste

Directions:

1. Combine the chopped fresh parsley, cilantro, and mint leaves in a mixing bowl.
2. Add the minced garlic and finely chopped red onion to the bowl.
3. Stir in the fresh lime juice and white vinegar to enhance the tangy flavour.
4. Drizzle the olive oil over the mixture and sprinkle the ground cumin.
5. Season the Salsa Verde with salt and pepper according to your preference.
6. Mix all the ingredients until well combined and the flavours are evenly distributed.
7. Use the Diabetic Salsa Verde immediately as a zesty and herbaceous topping for grilled fish, chicken, or vegetables. Alternatively, transfer the salsa verde to an airtight container and store it in the refrigerator for up to 3 days.
8. Serve the Salsa Verde as a delightful and diabetes-friendly condiment, offering fresh and tangy flavours to enhance your dishes.

Nutritional Information (per serving - 2 tablespoons):

- Calories: 20 kcal
- Carbohydrates: 1g
- Protein: 0g
- Fat: 2g
- Saturated Fat: 0.3g
- Fibre: 0g
- Sugar: 0.2g
- Sodium: 5mg

13. HUMMUS

Servings: 1 1/2 cups
Prep time: 10 minutes
Cooking time: 0 minutes

Ingredients:

- 1 can (400g) chickpeas, drained and rinsed
- 2 tablespoons tahini (sesame seed paste)
- 2 tablespoons fresh lemon juice
- 1 clove garlic, minced
- 1/2 teaspoon ground cumin
- 1/4 teaspoon paprika
- 2 tablespoons extra-virgin olive oil
- 2 tablespoons water
- Salt and pepper to taste

Directions:

1. Combine the drained and rinsed chickpeas, tahini, fresh lemon juice, minced garlic, ground cumin, and paprika in a food processor or blender.
2. Pulse the mixture until it breaks down and forms a coarse paste.
3. While the food processor is running, drizzle in the extra-virgin olive oil and water to create a smooth and creamy consistency. You may need to stop and scrape down the sides of the bowl a few times to ensure all the ingredients are well blended.
4. Taste the hummus and season with salt and pepper according to your preference. You can also adjust the amount of lemon juice, garlic, or spices to suit your taste.
5. Continue blending until the hummus reaches your desired texture. If it's too thick, add more water or olive oil to achieve the desired consistency.
6. Transfer the Diabetic Hummus to a serving bowl or an airtight container.
7. Serve the hummus immediately as a delicious and diabetes-friendly dip for vegetable sticks, whole-grain crackers, or pita bread. Alternatively, store the hummus in the refrigerator for up to 5 days.

Nutritional Information (per serving - 2 tablespoons):

- Calories: 50 kcal
- Carbohydrates: 4g
- Protein: 2g
- Fat: 3g
- Saturated Fat: 0.4g
- Fibre: 1g
- Sugar: 0.2g
- Sodium: 60mg

14. PESTO SAUCE

Servings: 1 cup
Prep time: 10 minutes
Cooking time: 0 minutes

Ingredients:

- 500g fresh basil leaves, packed
- 75g pine nuts (or walnuts for a nuttier taste)
- 75g grated Parmesan cheese
- 1 clove garlic, minced
- 125g extra-virgin olive oil
- 1 tablespoon fresh lemon juice
- Salt and pepper to taste

Directions:

1. Combine the fresh basil leaves, pine nuts, grated Parmesan cheese, and minced garlic in a food processor or blender.
2. Pulse the mixture until the ingredients break down and form a coarse paste.
3. While the food processor runs, slowly drizzle in the extra-virgin olive oil to create a smooth and creamy consistency. You may need to stop and scrape down the sides of the bowl a few times to ensure all the ingredients are well blended.
4. Add the fresh lemon juice to enhance the tangy flavour of the pesto sauce.
5. Taste the pesto sauce and season with salt and pepper according to your preference. Adjust the amount of garlic or cheese to suit your taste.
6. Continue blending until the pesto sauce reaches your desired texture. If it's too thick, add more olive oil to achieve the desired consistency.
7. Transfer the Diabetic Pesto Sauce to a serving bowl or an airtight container.
8. Serve the pesto sauce immediately as a delicious and diabetes-friendly topping for whole-grain pasta, zucchini noodles, grilled chicken, or fish. Alternatively, store the pesto sauce in the refrigerator for up to 5 days.

Nutritional Information (per serving - 2 tablespoons):

- Calories: 100 kcal
- Carbohydrates: 1g
- Protein: 1g
- Fat: 10g
- Saturated Fat: 1.5g
- Fibre: 0g
- Sugar: 0.1g
- Sodium: 40mg

15. TZATZIKI

Servings: 1 cup
Prep time: 15 minutes
Cooking time: 0 minutes

Ingredients:

- 250ml Greek yoghurt (low-fat or fat-free)
- 1/2 cucumber, grated and excess liquid squeezed out
- 1 clove garlic, minced
- 1 tablespoon fresh dill, chopped
- 1 tablespoon fresh mint, chopped
- 1 tablespoon fresh lemon juice
- 1 tablespoon extra-virgin olive oil
- Salt and pepper to taste

Directions:

1. Start by grating the cucumber and squeeze out the excess liquid using a clean kitchen towel or paper towel. This step prevents the Tzatziki from becoming too watery.
2. Combine the Greek yoghurt, grated cucumber, minced garlic, chopped dill, and chopped mint in a mixing bowl.
3. Stir in the fresh lemon juice and extra-virgin olive oil to enhance the flavour of the Tzatziki.
4. Season the Tzatziki with salt and pepper according to your preference.
5. Mix all the ingredients until well combined and the flavours are evenly distributed.
6. Taste the Tzatziki and adjust the seasonings or herbs as needed.
7. Transfer the Diabetic Tzatziki to a serving bowl or an airtight container.
8. Serve the Tzatziki immediately as a delicious and diabetes-friendly dip for vegetable sticks, whole-grain pita bread, or a topping for grilled chicken or fish. Alternatively, store the Tzatziki in the refrigerator for up to 3 days.

Nutritional Information (per serving - 2 tablespoons):

- Calories: 30 kcal
- Carbohydrates: 2g
- Protein: 2g
- Fat: 2g
- Saturated Fat: 0.3g
- Fibre: 0g
- Sugar: 1g
- Sodium: 10mg

16. SUGAR-FREE KETCHUP

Servings: 1 cup
Prep time: 5 minutes
Cooking time: 25 minutes

Ingredients:

- 1 can (400g) unsalted tomato sauce (no added sugar)
- 75ml apple cider vinegar
- 75ml water
- 1 tablespoon onion powder
- 1 teaspoon garlic powder
- 1/2 teaspoon ground cinnamon
- 1/4 teaspoon ground cloves
- 1/4 teaspoon ground allspice
- Salt and pepper to taste
- Liquid Stevia (or other sugar substitute) to taste

Directions:

1. Combine the unsalted tomato sauce, apple cider vinegar, and water in a medium-sized saucepan.
2. Stir in the onion powder, garlic powder, cinnamon, cloves, and allspice.
3. Season the mixture with salt and pepper according to your preference.
4. Bring the mixture to a gentle simmer over medium-low heat, stirring occasionally to prevent sticking.
5. Let the ketchup simmer for about 20-25 minutes or until it thickens to your desired consistency. Keep in mind that it will continue to thicken slightly as it cools.
6. Taste the ketchup and sweeten it with liquid Stevia or your preferred sugar substitute until it reaches your desired level of sweetness.
7. Remove the saucepan from the heat and let the ketchup cool to room temperature.
8. Transfer the Diabetic Sugar-Free Ketchup to a sterilized glass jar or an airtight container.
9. Store the ketchup in the refrigerator for up to 2 weeks.

Nutritional Information (per serving - 1 tablespoon):

- Calories: 5 kcal
- Carbohydrates: 1g
- Protein: 0.1g
- Fat: 0g
- Saturated Fat: 0g
- Fibre: 0.2g
- Sugar: 0.3g
- Sodium: 30mg

17. LOW-SODIUM SOY SAUCE

Servings: 1 cup
Prep time: 5 minutes
Cooking time: 10 minutes

Ingredients:

- 240ml reduced-sodium beef or vegetable broth (check for no added sugar)
- 2 tablespoons balsamic vinegar
- 1 tablespoon Worcestershire sauce (check for no added sugar)
- 1 teaspoon ground ginger
- 1 teaspoon garlic powder
- 1/4 teaspoon ground black pepper
- 1/4 teaspoon onion powder
- 1/4 teaspoon liquid Stevia (or other sugar substitute)
- 1 tablespoon cornstarch (or arrowroot powder) mixed with 2 tablespoons water

Directions:

1. Combine the reduced-sodium beef or vegetable broth in a saucepan with balsamic vinegar, Worcestershire sauce, ground ginger, garlic powder, black pepper, and onion powder.
2. Heat the mixture over medium heat, stirring occasionally.
3. Let the mixture come to a gentle simmer.
4. Add the liquid Stevia or your preferred sugar substitute to the mixture, adjusting the sweetness to your taste.
5. Mix the cornstarch (or arrowroot powder) in a separate small bowl with water to create a slurry.
6. Slowly add the slurry to the simmering mixture while stirring constantly. This will help thicken the sauce.
7. Simmering the sauce for about 5 minutes or until it thickens to the desired consistency.
8. Remove the saucepan from the heat and let the Low-Sodium Soy Sauce cool to room temperature.
9. Transfer the Diabetic Low-Sodium Soy Sauce to a sterilized glass jar or an airtight container.
10. Store the soy sauce in the refrigerator for up to 2 weeks.

Nutritional Information (per serving - 1 tablespoon):

- Calories: 5 kcal
- Carbohydrates: 1g
- Protein: 0.1g
- Fat: 0g
- Saturated Fat: 0g
- Fibre: 0g
- Sugar: 0.1g
- Sodium: 25mg

CHAPTER 8

DESERTS & SWEET TREATS

1. BERRY PARFAIT

Servings: 2
Prep time: 10 minutes
Cooking time: 0 minutes

Ingredients:

- 250ml plain Greek yoghurt (low-fat or fat-free)
- 1 teaspoon liquid Stevia (or other sugar substitute)
- 250g mixed fresh berries (strawberries, blueberries, raspberries)
- 2 tablespoons chopped nuts (e.g., almonds, walnuts, or pistachios)
- 2 tablespoons unsweetened shredded coconut
- Fresh mint leaves for garnish (optional)

Directions:

1. Mix the plain Greek yoghurt with liquid Stevia (or your preferred sugar substitute) in a small bowl to sweeten it. Adjust the sweetness according to your taste.
2. Rinse the fresh berries and gently pat them dry with a paper towel.
3. In two serving glasses or dessert bowls, start layering the parfait. Begin with a spoonful of sweetened Greek yoghurt.
4. Add a layer of mixed fresh berries on top of the yoghurt.
5. Sprinkle a tablespoon of chopped nuts over the berries.
6. Add another layer of sweetened Greek yoghurt.
7. Sprinkle another tablespoon of chopped nuts over the second layer of yoghurt.
8. Top each parfait with unsweetened shredded coconut for added texture and flavour.
9. Garnish with fresh mint leaves for an extra touch of freshness (optional).
10. Serve the Diabetic Berry Parfait immediately or refrigerate for 1 hour before serving.

Nutritional Information (per serving):

- Calories: 150 kcal
- Carbohydrates: 10g
- Protein: 8g
- Fat: 9g
- Saturated Fat: 3g
- Fibre: 3g
- Sugar: 6g
- Sodium: 30mg

2. BAKED APPLES

Servings: 4

Prep time: 15 minutes

Cooking time: 25 minutes

Ingredients:

- 4 medium-sized apples (e.g., Granny Smith, Pink Lady, or Honeycrisp)
- 1 tablespoon unsalted butter, melted
- 1 teaspoon ground cinnamon
- 1/4 teaspoon ground nutmeg
- 1/4 teaspoon ground ginger
- 1 tablespoon chopped walnuts or pecans
- 1 tablespoon raisins or dried cranberries (unsweetened)
- 2 tablespoons water
- Greek yoghurt (low-fat or fat-free) for serving (optional)

Directions:

1. Preheat your oven to 180°C (350°F) and grease a baking dish with non-stick cooking spray.
2. Wash the apples and pat them dry with a paper towel. Remove the cores from the apples using an apple corer or a small knife, creating a well in the centre.
3. Mix the melted unsalted butter in a small bowl with ground cinnamon, ground nutmeg, and ground ginger.
4. Brush the spiced butter mixture over the entire surface of each apple, ensuring they are well coated.
5. Place the chopped walnuts or pecans and the raisins or dried cranberries into the wells of the apples.
6. Arrange the stuffed apples in the greased baking dish and pour 2 tablespoons of water into the container to prevent the apples from sticking.
7. Bake the apples in the preheated oven for about 25 minutes or until tender and slightly caramelized.
8. Remove the baking dish from the oven and let the Baked Apples cool slightly before serving.
9. Optionally, serve the Baked Apples with a dollop of Greek yoghurt on top for added creaminess and protein.

Nutritional Information (per serving):

- Calories: 120 kcal
- Carbohydrates: 20g
- Protein: 1.5g
- Fat: 4.5g
- Saturated Fat: 1.5g
- Fibre: 4g
- Sugar: 13g
- Sodium: 5mg

3. CHIA SEED PUDDING

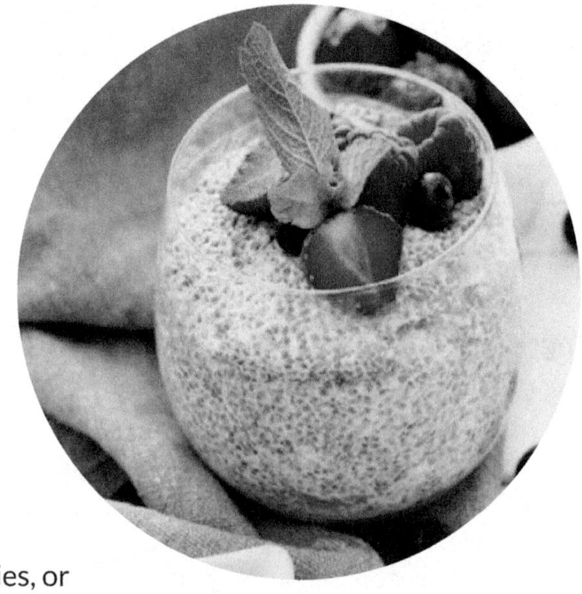

Servings: 2
Prep time: 5 minutes
Cooking time: 0 minutes (plus chilling time)

Ingredients:

- 75g chia seeds
- 250ml unsweetened almond milk (or any non-dairy milk of your choice)
- 1 teaspoon liquid Stevia (or other sugar substitute)
- 1/2 teaspoon vanilla extract
- Fresh berries for topping (e.g., strawberries, blueberries, or raspberries)

Directions:

1. Combine the chia seeds, unsweetened almond milk, liquid Stevia, and vanilla extract in a mixing bowl.
2. Stir the mixture thoroughly to ensure the chia seeds are well distributed and do not clump together.
3. Cover the bowl and refrigerate the mixture for at least 2 hours or overnight. During this time, the chia seeds will absorb the liquid and thicken to create a pudding-like consistency.
4. After chilling, stir the mixture well to ensure it is smooth and creamy.
5. Divide the Diabetic Chia Seed Pudding into serving bowls or glasses.
6. Top each serving with fresh berries for added natural sweetness and flavour.
7. Serve the Chia Seed Pudding immediately or refrigerate for up to 2 days.

Nutritional Information (per serving):

- Calories: 100 kcal
- Carbohydrates: 8g
- Protein: 4g
- Fat: 6g
- Saturated Fat: 0.5g
- Fibre: 7g
- Sugar: 0g
- Sodium: 70mg

4. SUGAR-FREE POPSICLES

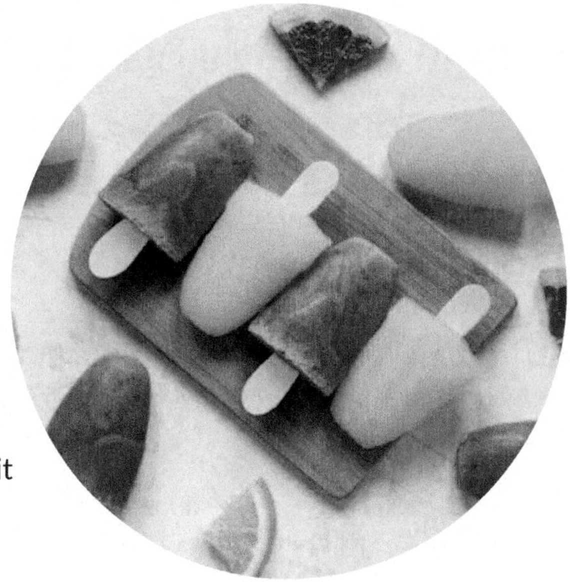

Servings: 6
Prep time: 10 minutes
Freeze Time: 4 hours (or until completely frozen)

Ingredients:

- 250g fresh berries (e.g., strawberries, blueberries, or raspberries)
- 250ml unsweetened apple juice (or any sugar-free fruit juice of your choice)
- 1 tablespoon freshly squeezed lemon juice
- 1 teaspoon liquid Stevia (or other sugar substitute)

Directions:

1. Rinse the fresh berries and pat them dry with a paper towel. Cut any large berries into smaller pieces for more effortless blending.
2. Combine the fresh berries, unsweetened apple juice, freshly squeezed lemon juice, and liquid Stevia in a blender or food processor.
3. Blend the mixture until it becomes smooth and well combined.
4. Taste the mixture and adjust the sweetness to your preference by adding more liquid Stevia if needed.
5. Pour the mixture into popsicle moulds, leaving a little space at the top to allow for expansion during freezing.
6. Insert popsicle sticks into each mould.
7. Place the popsicle moulds in the freezer and let them freeze for at least 4 hours or until completely frozen.
8. Once frozen, remove the popsicles from the moulds by running warm water over the outside for a few seconds to help release them.
9. Serve the Diabetic Sugar-Free Popsicles immediately or store them in an airtight container in the freezer for up to 2 weeks.

Nutritional Information (per popsicle):

- Calories: 25 kcal
- Carbohydrates: 6g
- Protein: 0.2g
- Fat: 0g
- Saturated Fat: 0g
- Fibre: 1.5g
- Sugar: 3g
- Sodium: 1mg

5. LEMON RICOTTA MOUSSE

Servings: 4
Prep time: 15 minutes
Chill Time: 2 hours

Ingredients:

- 250ml ricotta cheese (low-fat or fat-free)
- 75ml plain Greek yoghurt (low-fat or fat-free)
- Zest of 1 lemon
- 2 tablespoons freshly squeezed lemon juice
- 1 teaspoon liquid Stevia (or other sugar substitute)
- 1/2 teaspoon vanilla extract
- Fresh berries for topping (e.g., strawberries, blueberries, or raspberries)
- Fresh mint leaves for garnish (optional)

Directions:

1. Combine the ricotta cheese, plain Greek yoghurt, lemon zest, freshly squeezed lemon juice, liquid Stevia, and vanilla extract in a mixing bowl.
2. Use an electric mixer or a whisk to blend the mixture until it becomes smooth and creamy.
3. Taste the mixture and adjust the sweetness to your liking by adding more liquid Stevia if desired.
4. Cover the bowl with cling film and refrigerate the Lemon Ricotta Mousse for at least 2 hours to allow the flavours to meld and the mousse to chill.
5. After chilling, stir the mousse well to ensure it is well combined.
6. Divide the Diabetic Lemon Ricotta Mousse into serving glasses or dessert bowls.
7. Top each serving with fresh berries for added natural sweetness and a burst of colour.
8. Optionally, garnish with fresh mint leaves for an extra touch of freshness.
9. Serve the Lemon Ricotta Mousse immediately or refrigerate for up to 2 days.

Nutritional Information (per serving):

- Calories: 90 kcal
- Carbohydrates: 4g
- Protein: 7g
- Fat: 5g
- Saturated Fat: 3g
- Fibre: 0.5g
- Sugar: 2g
- Sodium: 50mg

1. SUGAR-FREE JELLO

Servings: 6
Prep time: 5 minutes
Chill Time: 4 hours (or until set)

Ingredients:

- 1 packet (0.3 oz or 8.5g) sugar-free gelatin (flavour of your choice)
- 480ml boiling water
- 240ml cold water
- Fresh berries for garnish (e.g., strawberries, blueberries, or raspberries)

Directions:

1. In a heatproof mixing bowl, empty the contents of the sugar-free gelatin packet.
2. Pour boiling water over the gelatin powder, and stir until the powder is completely dissolved.
3. Add cold water to the gelatin mixture and mix well.
4. Let the mixture sit for a few minutes to cool slightly.
5. Give the mixture a final stir to ensure it is well combined.
6. Pour the Diabetic Sugar-Free Jello mixture into serving cups or a large glass bowl.
7. Optionally, add fresh berries to add flavour and a pop of colour.
8. Cover the serving cups or bowl with cling film or a lid.
9. Refrigerate the Jello for at least 4 hours or until it is completely set.
10. Once set, remove the cling film or lid, and serve the Diabetic Sugar-Free Jello chilled.

Nutritional Information (per serving):

- Calories: 5 kcal
- Carbohydrates: 0g
- Protein: 1g
- Fat: 0g
- Saturated Fat: 0g
- Fibre: 0g
- Sugar: 0g
- Sodium: 30mg

1. FROZEN YOGURT BITES

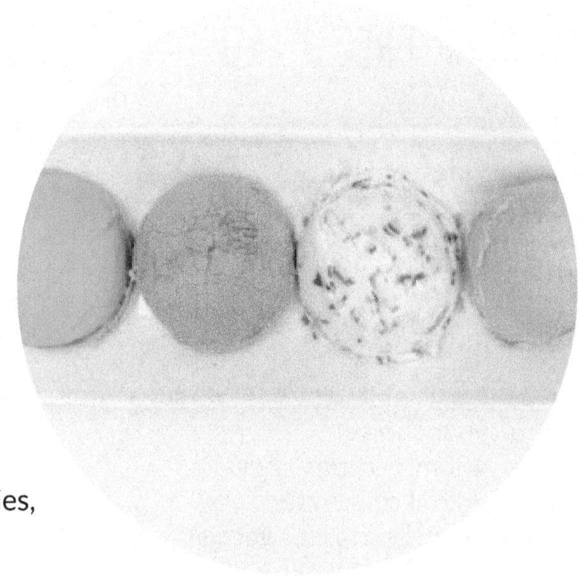

Servings: 12 (approximately)
Prep time: 10 minutes
Freeze Time: 2 hours (or until firm)

Ingredients:

- 250ml plain Greek yoghurt (low-fat or fat-free)
- 1 tablespoon liquid Stevia (or other sugar substitute)
- 1 teaspoon vanilla extract
- Fresh berries for topping (e.g., strawberries, blueberries, or raspberries)

Directions:

1. Combine the plain Greek yoghurt, liquid Stevia, and vanilla extract in a mixing bowl.
2. Stir the mixture until the sweetener is well incorporated and the yoghurt is smooth.
3. Line a mini muffin tin or a small baking tray with parchment paper or silicone liners.
4. Carefully spoon the yoghurt mixture into each muffin cup, filling them halfway.
5. Top each cup with fresh berries for added natural sweetness and flavour.
6. Place the muffin tin or baking tray in the freezer and let the Frozen Yogurt Bites set for at least 2 hours or until they are firm.
7. Once the bites are completely frozen, remove them from the muffin tin or tray.
8. Transfer the Frozen Yogurt Bites to an airtight container and store them in the freezer for up to 2 weeks.
9. Serve the Diabetic Frozen Yogurt Bites chilled as a delightful and guilt-free dessert or snack.

Nutritional Information (per serving, 1 yoghurt bite):

- Calories: 10 kcal
- Carbohydrates: 1g
- Protein: 1g
- Fat: 0g
- Saturated Fat: 0g
- Fibre: 0g
- Sugar: 0g
- Sodium: 5mg

1. PEANUT BUTTER ENERGY BALLS

Servings: 12 energy balls
Prep time: 15 minutes
Chill Time: 30 minutes (optional)

Ingredients:

- 250g rolled oats
- 125g natural peanut butter (sugar-free, no added oil)
- 75g ground flaxseed
- 75g unsweetened shredded coconut
- 2 tablespoons unsweetened cocoa powder
- 2 tablespoons liquid Stevia (or other sugar substitute)
- 1 teaspoon vanilla extract
- Pinch of salt
- 2-3 tablespoons water (if needed for consistency)

Directions:

1. Combine the rolled oats, natural peanut butter, ground flaxseed, unsweetened shredded coconut, unsweetened cocoa powder, liquid Stevia, vanilla extract, and a pinch of salt in a large mixing bowl.
2. Mix all the ingredients thoroughly until well combined. The mixture should be sticky enough to hold its shape when pressed together. If it's too dry, add a little water (1 tablespoon at a time) until you achieve the desired consistency.
3. Once the mixture is ready, take a small portion and roll it between your palms to form a compact ball. Repeat this process until all the mixture is used, making approximately 12 energy balls.
4. Optional: Refrigerate the energy balls for about 30 minutes for a firmer texture.
5. Store the Diabetic Peanut Butter Energy Balls in an airtight container in the refrigerator for up to 1 week.

Nutritional Information (per energy ball):

- Calories: 85 kcal
- Carbohydrates: 7g
- Protein: 3g
- Fat: 5g
- Saturated Fat: 1g
- Fibre: 2g
- Sugar: 0.5g
- Sodium: 30mg

1. ALMOND FLOUR COOKIES

Servings: 12 cookies
Prep time: 15 minutes
Bake Time: 12-15 minutes

Ingredients:

- 250g almond flour
- 2 tablespoons coconut oil, melted
- 2 tablespoons liquid Stevia (or other sugar substitute)
- 1 teaspoon vanilla extract
- 1/4 teaspoon baking soda
- Pinch of salt
- 75g sugar-free dark chocolate chips (optional)

Directions:

1. Preheat your oven to 180°C (350°F) and line a baking tray with parchment paper.
2. Combine the almond flour, melted coconut oil, liquid Stevia, vanilla extract, baking soda, and a pinch of salt in a mixing bowl. Mix until a dough forms.
3. If you prefer your cookies to be sweeter, add more liquid Stevia according to your taste.
4. Optionally, fold in the sugar-free dark chocolate chips for added texture and sweetness.
5. Roll small portions of the cookie dough between your palms to form 12 evenly-sized balls.
6. Place the cookie balls on the prepared baking tray and gently flatten them with your fingers.
7. Bake the Almond Flour Cookies in the oven for 12-15 minutes or until the edges turn golden brown.
8. Remove the cookies from the oven and let them cool on the baking tray for a few minutes.
9. Transfer the cookies to a wire rack to cool completely.
10. Once cooled, store the Diabetic Almond Flour Cookies in an airtight container for up to 5 days.

Nutritional Information (per cookie):

- Calories: 70 kcal
- Carbohydrates: 2.5g
- Protein: 1.5g
- Fat: 6g
- Saturated Fat: 2g
- Fibre: 1g
- Sugar: 0.5g
- Sodium: 30mg

1. CINNAMON ROASTED ALMONDS

Servings: 2 cups
Prep time: 5 minutes
Roast Time: 15 minutes

Ingredients:

- 500g raw almonds
- 1 tablespoon coconut oil, melted
- 1 teaspoon ground cinnamon
- 1/2 teaspoon vanilla extract
- Pinch of salt
- 1 tablespoon liquid Stevia (or other sugar substitute)

Directions:

1. Preheat your oven to 160°C (320°F) and line a baking tray with parchment paper.
2. Combine the raw almonds, melted coconut oil, ground cinnamon, vanilla extract, and a pinch of salt in a mixing bowl. Mix well to coat the almonds evenly.
3. If you prefer the almonds to be sweeter, add the liquid Stevia and mix to distribute it evenly.
4. Spread the coated almonds in a single layer on the prepared baking tray.
5. Roast the Cinnamon Roasted Almonds in the oven for 15 minutes, stirring halfway through to ensure even roasting.
6. Remove the almonds from the oven and let them cool on the baking tray for a few minutes.
7. Transfer the cooled almonds to an airtight container and store them at room temperature for up to 2 weeks.

Nutritional Information (per 1-ounce serving):

- Calories: 160 kcal
- Carbohydrates: 5g
- Protein: 5g
- Fat: 14g
- Saturated Fat: 2g
- Fibre: 3g
- Sugar: 1g
- Sodium: 20mg

1. SUGAR-FREE CHEESECAKE

Servings: 8 servings

Prep time: 20 minutes

Chill Time: 4 hours (or overnight)

Ingredients: For the crust:

- 250g almond flour
- 2 tablespoons unsweetened cocoa powder
- 2 tablespoons coconut oil, melted
- 1 tablespoon liquid Stevia (or other sugar substitute)
- Pinch of salt
- For the filling:
- 500g cream cheese, softened (low-fat or full-fat)
- 120ml plain Greek yoghurt (low-fat or fat-free)
- 2 large eggs
- 1 teaspoon vanilla extract
- Zest of 1 lemon
- 1 tablespoon lemon juice
- 60ml liquid Stevia (or other sugar substitute)

Directions:

1. Preheat your oven to 160°C (320°F), grease a 7-inch springform pan with coconut oil, or line it with parchment paper.
2. Mix the almond flour, unsweetened cocoa powder, melted coconut oil, liquid Stevia, and a pinch of salt to make the crust in a mixing bowl. Mix until the mixture resembles wet sand.
3. Press the crust mixture firmly into the bottom of the prepared springform pan to form an even layer.
4. In a separate mixing bowl, beat the softened cream cheese and plain Greek yoghurt until smooth and creamy.
5. Add the eggs, one at a time, beating well after each addition.
6. Mix in the vanilla extract, lemon zest, lemon juice, and liquid Stevia until well combined.
7. Pour the filling over the crust in the springform pan and spread it evenly.
8. Bake the Sugar-Free Cheesecake in the oven for 40-45 minutes or until the edges are set and the centre is slightly jiggly.
9. Turn off the oven and leave the cheesecake inside for 1 hour to cool slowly.
10. Remove the cheesecake from the oven and let it cool at room temperature.
11. Once cooled, refrigerate the cheesecake for at least 4 hours or overnight to firm up.
12. Before serving, you can garnish the cheesecake with fresh berries or a dusting of cocoa powder if desired.

Nutritional Information (per serving):

- Calories: 250 kcal
- Carbohydrates: 5g
- Protein: 7g
- Fat: 22g
- Saturated Fat: 11g
- Fibre: 2g
- Sugar: 1g
- Sodium: 250mg

1. BAKED PEARS WITH CINNAMON

Servings: 4
Prep time: 10 minutes
Bake Time: 25 minutes

Ingredients:

- 4 ripe pears (such as Bartlett or Anjou)
- 1 tablespoon unsalted butter, melted
- 1 tablespoon liquid Stevia (or other sugar substitute)
- 1 teaspoon ground cinnamon
- Optional toppings:
- Plain Greek yoghurt (low-fat or fat-free)
- Chopped nuts (such as almonds or walnuts)
- Drizzle of honey (optional, adjust to taste)

Directions:

1. Preheat your oven to 180°C (350°F) and grease a baking dish with a little butter.
2. Wash and halve the pears. Remove the cores and seeds with a spoon, creating a small cavity in each pear half.
3. Mix the melted unsalted butter and liquid Stevia in a small bowl.
4. Brush the cut side of each pear half with the butter and Stevia mixture.
5. Sprinkle ground cinnamon over the brushed side of the pears.
6. Place the pear halves in the greased baking dish, cut side up.
7. Bake the Baked Pears with Cinnamon in the oven for 25 minutes or until the pears are tender and slightly caramelized.
8. Once baked, remove the pears from the oven and let them cool for a few minutes.
9. Optionally, serve the Baked Pears with a dollop of plain Greek yoghurt and a sprinkling of chopped nuts.
10. You can drizzle a little honey over the pears for added sweetness, adjusting the amount according to your taste.

Nutritional Information (per serving, without optional toppings):

- Calories: 90 kcal
- Carbohydrates: 18g
- Protein: 1g
- Fat: 2g
- Saturated Fat: 1g
- Fibre: 4g
- Sugar: 10g
- Sodium: 0mg

1. VANILLA PANNA COTTA

Servings: 4
Prep time: 10 minutes
Chill Time: 4 hours (or overnight)

Ingredients:

- 400ml unsweetened almond milk (or other milk of choice)
- 2 teaspoons powdered gelatin
- 1 teaspoon vanilla extract
- 2 tablespoons liquid Stevia (or other sugar substitute)
- Fresh berries or sugar-free fruit compote for serving (optional)

Directions:

1. In a small bowl, sprinkle the powdered gelatin over 50ml of cold water. Allow it to bloom for about 5 minutes.
2. In a saucepan, gently warm the unsweetened almond milk over low heat. Add the liquid Stevia and stir until dissolved.
3. Remove the saucepan from the heat and stir in the bloomed gelatin mixture until completely dissolved.
4. Stir in the vanilla extract to infuse the milk with a delightful vanilla flavour.
5. Allow the mixture to cool slightly before pouring into individual serving cups or ramekins.
6. Refrigerate the Vanilla Panna Cotta cups for at least 4 hours or preferably overnight until set.
7. Before serving, top the Panna Cotta with fresh berries or a sugar-free fruit compote for added sweetness and a burst of flavour.

Nutritional Information (per serving, without toppings):

- Calories: 30 kcal
- Carbohydrates: 1g
- Protein: 2g
- Fat: 2g
- Saturated Fat: 0g
- Fibre: 0g
- Sugar: 0g
- Sodium: 80mg

CHAPTER 9

BEVERAGES

1. HERBAL TEAS

Servings: 1 cup
Prep time: 5 minutes
Steeping Time: 5-10 minutes

Ingredients:

- 1 teaspoon dried herbs of your choice (e.g., peppermint, chamomile, hibiscus, ginger, cinnamon, rooibos, lemon balm)
- 250ml boiling water
- Optional sweeteners:
- Liquid Stevia (or other sugar substitute) to taste
- Lemon or lime slices (for a citrusy twist)

Directions:

1. Boil water in a kettle or saucepan.
2. Place the dried herbs in a tea infuser or a tea bag. If using loose spices, you can also use a filter.
3. Pour the boiling water over the herbs in your teacup.
4. Allow the herbal tea to steep for 5-10 minutes, depending on the type of herbs and your desired strength.
5. If you prefer a sweeter taste, you can add liquid Stevia or any other sugar substitute of your choice, adjusting the amount according to your taste preference.
6. Optionally, you can enhance the flavour by adding a slice of lemon or lime for a refreshing citrusy twist.
7. Stir the tea well, remove the tea infuser or tea bag, and enjoy your delightful and diabetes-friendly Herbal Tea.

2. GREEN TEA

Servings: 1 cup
Prep time: 2 minutes
Steeping Time: 3-5 minutes

Ingredients:

- 1 green tea bag (or 1 teaspoon of loose green tea leaves)
- 250ml boiling water
- Optional additions:
- Liquid Stevia (or other sugar substitute) to taste
- Fresh lemon slices (for added zest)

Directions:

1. Boil water in a kettle or saucepan.
2. Place the green tea bag or loose green tea leaves in your teacup.
3. Pour the boiling water over the tea in the cup.
4. Allow the green tea to steep for 3-5 minutes, depending on your desired strength. Steep for a shorter time for a milder flavour or a longer time for a more pungent taste.
5. After steeping, remove the tea bag or strain the tea leaves from the cup.
6. If you prefer a sweeter taste, you can add liquid Stevia or any other sugar substitute to your liking.
7. Optionally, you can enhance the flavour by adding a slice of fresh lemon for a zesty and refreshing twist.
8. Stir the tea well, and enjoy your diabetes-friendly Green Tea.

3. BLACK COFFEE

Servings: 1 cup
Prep time: 1 minute
Brew Time: 5 minutes

Ingredients:

- 1 tablespoon ground coffee (medium-coarse grind)
- 250ml hot water
- Optional additions:
- Unsweetened almond milk or soy milk (to taste)
- Liquid Stevia (or other sugar substitute) to taste

Directions:

1. Boil water in a kettle or saucepan until it reaches the desired temperature for brewing.
2. Place 1 tablespoon of medium-coarse ground coffee into a coffee filter or a French press.
3. Pour the hot water over the ground coffee and allow it to steep for about 5 minutes. Adjust the steeping time to suit your preferred coffee strength.
4. After the brewing time, use a coffee filter or press down the plunger of the French press to separate the coffee grounds from the liquid.
5. Add a splash of unsweetened almond milk or soy milk to give your coffee a creamy touch.
6. Add liquid Stevia or any other sugar substitute to your liking for a sweeter taste without added sugar.
7. Stir well and savour your diabetes-friendly Black Coffee.

4. ICED TEA

Servings: 4
Prep time: 5 minutes
Brew Time: 5 minutes
Chill Time: 1-2 hours

Ingredients:

- 1000ml water
- 4 black tea bags (or tea bags of your choice)
- Ice cubes
- Fresh lemon slices (optional, for garnish)
- Liquid Stevia (or other sugar substitute) to taste (optional)

Directions:

1. Bring water to a boil in a kettle or saucepan.
2. Once the water is boiling, add the 4 black tea bags and allow them to steep for 5 minutes. Adjust the steeping time to achieve your preferred tea strength.
3. After the brewing time, remove the tea bags and discard them.
4. Allow the brewed tea to cool to room temperature.
5. Transfer the cooled tea to the refrigerator and let it chill for 1-2 hours.
6. When ready to serve, fill glasses with ice cubes.
7. Pour the chilled tea over the ice cubes.
8. Add a splash of fresh lemon juice for a zesty kick and extra refreshing taste if desired.
9. Add liquid Stevia or any other sugar substitute to your liking for a sweeter taste without added sugar.
10. Stir well and garnish with lemon slices if using.
11. Enjoy your delightful diabetes-friendly Iced Tea.

5. INFUSED WATER

Servings: 1 pitcher (approximately 8 cups)
Prep time: 5 minutes
Infusing Time: 1-2 hours

Ingredients:

- 1 pitcher of water (about 2L)
- Fresh fruits (e.g., strawberries, lemons, limes, oranges) - washed and sliced
- Fresh herbs (e.g., mint, basil) - washed and lightly crushed
- Ice cubes

Directions:

1. Take a clean pitcher and fill it with approximately 2L of water.
2. Add your desired combination of fresh fruits and herbs to the water. For example, you can use sliced strawberries, lemon, lime, orange, and a few sprigs of fresh mint or basil.
3. Gently crush the herbs between your fingers to release their flavours.
4. Place the pitcher of water in the refrigerator to infuse for 1-2 hours. The longer it invests, the stronger the flavours will become.
5. Before serving, add some ice cubes to the infused water for a refreshing chill.
6. Pour the infused water into glasses and enjoy your delightful, diabetes-friendly Infused Water.

6. SUGAR-FREE LEMONADE

Servings: 4
Prep time: 10 minutes
Cooking time: 0 minutes

Ingredients:

- 1L water
- Juice of 4 fresh lemons (approximately 250ml)
- Liquid Stevia (or other sugar substitute) to taste
- Ice cubes
- Fresh lemon slices and mint leaves for garnish (optional)

Directions:

1. Combine water with the freshly squeezed lemon juice in a pitcher. Stir well to mix.
2. Add liquid Stevia or your preferred sugar substitute to the lemon-water mixture. Start with a small amount and adjust to your desired sweetness level. Remember that Stevia is significantly sweeter than sugar, so a little goes a long way.
3. Taste the lemonade and add more sweetener if needed. Remember that the sweetness can vary depending on the tartness of the lemons.
4. Fill glasses with ice cubes.
5. Pour the sugar-free lemonade over the ice cubes.
6. Garnish with fresh lemon slices and a few mint leaves for an extra refreshing touch if desired.
7. Stir well and enjoy your delicious diabetes-friendly Sugar-Free Lemonade.

7. CUCUMBER MINT COOLER

Servings: 2
Prep time: 10 minutes
Cooking time: 0 minutes

Ingredients:

- 1 large cucumber, peeled and sliced
- 1 handful of fresh mint leaves
- 500ml cold water
- Juice of 1 lime
- Liquid Stevia (or other sugar substitute) to taste
- Ice cubes
- Cucumber slices and mint sprigs for garnish (optional)

Directions:

1. Combine the peeled and sliced cucumber with the fresh mint leaves in a blender or food processor.
2. Blend until the cucumber and mint are well pureed.
3. Strain the cucumber-mint mixture through a fine-mesh sieve into a pitcher to remove any solids.
4. Add cold water and the juice of 1 lime to the pitcher and stir well to combine.
5. Sweeten the cucumber mint cooler with liquid Stevia or your preferred sugar substitute. Start with a small amount and adjust to your desired sweetness.
6. Taste the cooler and add more sweetener if needed.
7. Fill two glasses with ice cubes.
8. Pour the cucumber mint cooler over the ice cubes.
9. Garnish with cucumber slices and a sprig of mint for an extra refreshing look if desired.
10. Stir well and enjoy your delicious diabetes-friendly Cucumber Mint Cooler.

8. HOMEMADE SMOOTHIES

Servings: 2
Prep time: 10 minutes
Cooking time: 0 minutes

Ingredients:

- 250ml unsweetened almond milk (or any non-dairy milk of your choice)
- 125ml plain Greek yoghurt
- 250g mixed berries (such as strawberries, blueberries, and raspberries)
- 1 small banana
- 1 tablespoon chia seeds
- 1/2 teaspoon pure vanilla extract
- Liquid Stevia (or other sugar substitute) to taste
- Ice cubes

Directions:

1. Add unsweetened almond milk, plain Greek yoghurt, mixed berries, banana, chia seeds, and pure vanilla extract in a blender.
2. Blend all the ingredients until smooth and well combined.
3. Taste the smoothie and add liquid Stevia or your preferred sugar substitute to reach your desired level of sweetness. Keep in mind that the sweetness of the smoothie will depend on the ripeness of the banana and the sweetness of the berries.
4. Blend again to incorporate the sweetener.
5. If the smoothie is too thick, add a few ice cubes and blend until you reach your desired consistency.
6. Pour the smoothie into two glasses.
7. Garnish with some fresh berries or a sprig of mint if desired.
8. Serve immediately and enjoy your diabetes-friendly Homemade Smoothies.

CHAPTER 10. MEAL PLANNING AND PORTION CONTROL

A. TIPS FOR DIABETIC MEAL PLANNING

Planning diabetic-friendly meals is essential for managing blood sugar levels and maintaining overall health. Here are some tips for effective diabetic meal planning:

- Choose Whole Foods: Opt for whole, unprocessed foods such as vegetables, fruits, lean proteins, whole grains, nuts, and seeds. These foods are rich in nutrients and have a lower impact on blood sugar levels.
- Control Carbohydrate Intake: Pay attention to the portion sizes and types of carbohydrates you consume. Aim for complex carbohydrates with a lower glycemic index, like whole grains, legumes, and non-starchy vegetables.
- Include Healthy Fats: Incorporate sources of healthy fats, such as avocados, nuts, seeds, and olive oil, in your meals. Fats can help slow down the absorption of sugar and promote satiety.
- Watch Portion Sizes: Portion control is crucial for managing blood sugar levels. Be mindful of portion sizes and avoid overeating, even with healthier food choices.
- Balance Macronutrients: Aim to include a balance of carbohydrates, proteins, and fats in each meal. This can help prevent rapid spikes in blood sugar levels.
- Limit Added Sugars: Avoid or minimize added sugars and sugary drinks. Choose natural sweeteners like Stevia, or use fruit to add sweetness to recipes.
- Plan Regular Meals: Consistency in meal timing can help regulate blood sugar levels. Aim for three balanced meals and one or two snacks daily.
- Include Fiber-Rich Foods: High-fiber foods like vegetables, fruits, whole grains, and legumes can help slow down the absorption of sugar and improve blood sugar control.
- Monitor Carbohydrate Intake: If you use insulin or other medications to manage diabetes, work with a healthcare professional to determine the appropriate carbohydrate intake.
- Be Mindful of Alcohol: Limit alcohol consumption and choose lower-sugar options if you do drink. Alcohol can affect blood sugar levels and interact with diabetes medications.
- Stay Hydrated: Drink plenty of water throughout the day to stay hydrated and support overall health.
- Experiment with Recipes: Try new diabetic-friendly recipes and experiment with different ingredients to keep meals exciting and enjoyable.
- Consider Glycemic Load: Pay attention to the glycemic load of foods, which considers both the glycemic index and portion size. Lower glycemic load foods have a milder impact on blood sugar levels.
- Read Labels: Be mindful of hidden sugars and carbohydrates by reading food labels carefully.
- Monitor Blood Sugar: Keep track of your blood sugar levels regularly and adjust your meal plan if necessary.

Remember, individual needs may vary, so it's essential to work with a registered dietitian or healthcare professional to create a personalized diabetic meal plan that meets your specific health goals and preferences.

B. UNDERSTANDING CARBOHYDRATE COUNTING

Carbohydrate counting is a method used by diabetics to manage their blood sugar levels by closely monitoring the amount of carbohydrates they consume in their meals. Carbohydrates are the primary macronutrient that directly affects blood sugar levels, as they break down into glucose, the body's primary energy source.

Here's a step-by-step guide to understanding carbohydrate counting for diabetics:

1. Learn about Carbohydrates: Carbohydrates are found in various foods, including grains, fruits, vegetables, legumes, dairy products, and sweets. They are classified into three main types: sugars, starches, and fibres.
2. Identify Carbohydrate Sources: Get familiar with common carbohydrate-containing foods and their portion sizes. Remember that different foods can have varying amounts of carbohydrates per serving.
3. Read Food Labels: Pay attention to the nutrition labels on packaged foods to determine the total carbohydrate content per serving. Look for the "Total Carbohydrates" section, which includes both sugars and dietary fibre.
4. Measure Portions: Accurately measure the portion sizes of carbohydrate-rich foods you consume. This will help you calculate the total number of grams of carbohydrates you're eating.
5. Calculate Carbohydrate Content: Add up the total grams of carbohydrates from each food item to determine the overall carbohydrate content of your meal.
6. Understand Glycemic Index: The glycemic index (GI) ranks foods based on how quickly they raise blood sugar levels. Foods with a high GI are more likely to cause rapid spikes in blood sugar. Consider the GI of foods when planning meals.
7. Determine Insulin-to-Carbohydrate Ratio (ICR): If you use insulin to manage diabetes, work with your healthcare team to establish your insulin-to-carbohydrate ratio. This ratio helps determine how much insulin you need to cover the carbohydrates you consume.
8. Track Carbohydrate Intake: Keep a food diary or use a smartphone app to track your carbohydrate intake at each meal. This will help you monitor your blood sugar levels and adjust as needed.
9. Be Mindful of Sugar and Fiber: Pay attention to added sugars in foods, as they can affect blood sugar levels. Also, include high-fibre foods in your meals, as fibre can slow down glucose absorption.
10. Adjust as Needed: Monitor your blood sugar levels regularly and work with your healthcare team to adjust your carbohydrate counting plan if necessary.

C. CONTROLLING PORTION SIZES FOR BETTER BLOOD SUGAR MANAGEMENT

Controlling portion sizes is critical to blood sugar management for individuals with diabetes. Here are some practical tips to help diabetics control portion sizes and maintain stable blood sugar levels:

- Use smaller plates and bowls: Opt for smaller dishware to help visually control portion sizes and prevent overeating.
- Measure food portions: Use measuring cups, spoons, and a scale to measure ingredients and servings accurately.
- Read food labels: Pay attention to serving sizes and total carbohydrate content listed on food packaging.
- Divide your plate: Use the plate method to portion your meals. Fill half your plate with non-starchy vegetables, one-quarter with lean protein, and one-quarter with complex carbohydrates.
- Avoid second helpings: Pause for seconds to assess if you are hungry.
- Choose high-fibre foods: Foods high in fibre can help you feel fuller for longer and may help stabilize blood sugar levels.
- Be mindful of snacks: Portion snacks in advance to avoid mindless eating and monitor carbohydrate intake between meals.
- Limit liquid calories: Beverages like sodas, fruit juices, and sweetened drinks can quickly increase blood sugar levels. Choose water, unsweetened tea, or sugar-free options instead.
- Control portion sizes when eating out: Share large entrees or take half of the meal home for later.
- Listen to your body: Pay attention to hunger and fullness cues. Eat slowly and stop eating when you feel satisfied, not overly full.
- Avoid distractions: Avoid eating while watching TV or using electronic devices, as it can lead to overeating.
- Plan your meals: Plan your meals and snacks to avoid impulsive eating and make healthier choices.
- Be cautious with condiments and toppings: Be mindful of the amount of sauces, dressings, and toppings you use, as they can add extra calories and carbohydrates.
- Focus on nutrient-dense foods: Choose foods that provide essential nutrients without excess calories, such as fruits, vegetables, lean proteins, and whole grains.
- Work with a dietitian: Consult a registered dietitian who can create a personalized meal plan and guide portion control.

Everyone's dietary needs and preferences are different, so finding the proper portion control strategies that work for you is essential for maintaining stable blood sugar levels and overall health.

CHAPTER 11. CONCLUSION

A. SUMMARY OF CRUCIAL POINTS FOR DIABETIC COOKING

- Control Carbohydrates: Monitor and manage carbohydrate intake to regulate blood sugar levels. Focus on complex carbohydrates and avoid refined sugars and processed foods.
- Choose Nutrient-Dense Foods: Opt for foods rich in vitamins, minerals, and fibre to support overall health and manage blood sugar effectively.
- Portion Control: Be mindful of portion sizes to avoid overeating and maintain stable blood sugar levels.
- Emphasize Lean Proteins: Include lean protein sources in your meals to promote satiety and stabilize blood sugar levels.
- Healthy Fats: Choose heart-healthy fats such as avocados, nuts, and olive oil in moderation to support overall health.
- Limit Sodium: Reduce salt intake to manage blood pressure and overall health.
- Fibre Intake: Incorporate fibre-rich foods like whole grains, fruits, and vegetables to help regulate blood sugar levels and promote digestive health.
- Meal Planning: Plan balanced meals and snacks to make healthier food choices and avoid impulsive eating.
- Read Food Labels: Check nutrition labels for total carbohydrates, fibre, and added sugars to make informed food choices.
- Avoid Processed Foods: Minimize consumption of processed and high-sugar foods as they can negatively impact blood sugar levels.
- Stay Hydrated: Drink plenty of water throughout the day to stay hydrated and support overall health.
- Monitor Blood Sugar Levels: Regularly monitor blood sugar levels and adjust your diet.
- Exercise: Combine a healthy diet with regular physical activity to support blood sugar management and overall well-being.
- Work with a Healthcare Professional: Consult a healthcare provider or a registered dietitian to create a personalized diabetic meal plan and receive guidance tailored to your needs.

B. ENCOURAGEMENT FOR A HEALTHY AND ENJOYABLE DIABETIC LIFESTYLE

Living a healthy and satisfying diabetic lifestyle is entirely possible, and with determination and support, you can achieve your health goals and maintain a fulfilling life. Here's some encouragement to help you on your journey:

- Embrace Positive Changes: Every step you take towards a healthier lifestyle is a victory. Celebrate your progress, no matter how small, and remember that each positive choice makes a difference.

- Focus on What You Can Do: Instead of dwelling on limitations, focus on the vast array of delicious and nutritious foods you can enjoy. Explore new recipes and discover the joy of cooking and eating healthy meals.
- Learn and Educate: Knowledge is power. Take the time to understand how food affects your blood sugar levels and learn about diabetic-friendly ingredients and meal planning. Share your knowledge with friends and family to foster a supportive environment.
- Seek Support: Don't hesitate to seek support from healthcare professionals, diabetes support groups, or online communities. Surround yourself with people who understand and encourage your journey.
- Stay Active: Regular physical activity is essential for diabetes management and overall well-being. Find activities you enjoy, whether walking, swimming, dancing, or yoga, and make them part of your routine.
- Mindful Eating: Practice mindful eating by savouring each bite, listening to your body's hunger and fullness cues, and being present during meals. This can help you make healthier choices and enjoy your food more thoroughly.
- Treat Yourself: Occasional indulgences are a part of life. Allow yourself a treat now and then, and remember that balance is vital to a sustainable healthy lifestyle.
- Celebrate Achievements: Celebrate your successes, no matter how big or small. Whether reaching a fitness goal or managing your blood sugar levels effectively, acknowledge and reward yourself for your efforts.
- Focus on Overall Well-being: Remember that a healthy diabetic lifestyle extends beyond diet. Prioritize sleep, manage stress, and care for your mental and emotional well-being.
- Be Patient with Yourself: Managing diabetes is a journey, and there will be ups and downs. Be patient, and don't be too hard on yourself if you face challenges.
- Set Realistic Goals: Set achievable and realistic goals for yourself. Breaking down your larger goals into smaller, manageable steps can make them more attainable.
- Embrace Variety: Experiment with new foods, recipes, and activities. Variety keeps things exciting and helps you discover what works best for you.

C. INVITATION TO SHARE FEEDBACK AND RECIPES WITH THE COMMUNITY

We hope this message finds you in good health and high spirits! We are thrilled to be a part of this supportive and empowering community, where we share our journeys towards a healthier and enjoyable diabetic lifestyle.

Your feedback is invaluable to us. We would love to hear about your experiences, challenges, and triumphs in managing diabetes through diet and lifestyle. Whether you've discovered a new delicious recipe, found a helpful tip for blood sugar management, or have a heartwarming story to share, we encourage you to join the conversation.

Let's unite to inspire and uplift each other on this path to well-being. By sharing our knowledge and experiences, we can learn from one another and make our diabetic journey even more rewarding.

If you have any diabetic-friendly recipes that have become your go-to favourites, please share them with the community. Food can be both nutritious and delicious; your recipes might be what someone else needs to brighten up their mealtime.

To share your feedback, stories, and recipes, reply to this message or join our community forum. Together, we can positively impact and create a supportive space for everyone with diabetes.

Thank you for being a part of this beautiful community, and we look forward to connecting with you all.

Wishing you good health and happiness,

Printed in Great Britain
by Amazon

27325593R00084